Praise for *The No-Limits Enterprise*

"If you've been thinking that endless bureaucracy, red tape, and hierarchy is a terrible way to run a business, then you're exactly right. Read this book and learn exactly how to make your organization happier, freer, and more successful."

—Alexander Kjerulf

Chief Happiness Officer, Woohoo Inc.
Author and Speaker

"We can no longer talk about self-management as the 'future of work.' In his new book, Doug eloquently shows us all why it is the 'now of work.' This book should be compulsory reading for students of management and business leaders alike—anyone who wants to know what it takes to lead a company into the next decade."

—Evan Leybourn

Founder, Business Agility Institute

"Doug Kirkpatrick has done it again! *The No-Limits Enterprise* is your roadmap to the principles of self-management that have proven track records across the globe. He has turned the simplest of human traits—the desire to create with dedication and love—into a disciplined, transformative, and powerful new approach to building your company. All by leveraging the limitless power, passions, and commitments of your workforce. Get this book now!"

—Bill Jensen

Author, **Future Strong and Disrupt!**

"*The No-Limits Enterprise* is a timely, thought-provoking book. With its tools, templates, stories, and cases, it can help business leaders on the journey to organizational transformation from old and hierarchical to new and more empowering ways of working. This book deserves to be widely read!"

—Professor Vlatka Hlupic

Award-Winning Author, The Management Shift and Humane Capital

"In his new book *The No-Limits Enterprise*, Doug Kirkpatrick brings us a powerful message from the not-so-distant future: the only businesses with the speed and agility to lead markets and change industries will be the ones that can break free from the unbearable burden of bureaucracy through self-management."

—Josh Levine

Author, Great Mondays: How to Design a Company Culture Employees Love

"Are you on the verge of a bureaucratic breakdown? Can you Leahy? Doug Kirkpatrick offers a roadmap to the sanity, respect, and vitality of self-managed organizations. If you fail to read this book you do so at your own, and your organization's, peril—and you won't learn to Leahy."

—David Zinger

Founder and Host, Employee Experience & Engagement Network

"Finally! A comprehensive guide for anyone interested in self-management. Brought to you by one of the few true, no-nonsense experts in a field full of opportunistic charlatans and con artists."

—Pim de Morree

Cofounder, Corporate Rebels

"Doug really gets it. Where other academics and consultants talk about it, he's lived it. A true self-management pioneer. And this book not only reveals the founding principles of self-management, it gives you the tools and the guidance to implement it."

—Ray Hebert

Serial Entrepreneur and Business Innovator

"In a world of constant change, what is often overlooked is the organization as a whole. Doug is absolutely the right person to guide leaders in this realm. Get this book so you can give your team and all of your stakeholders the tools they want to really thrive."

—R. Michael Anderson

Bestselling Author, **Soul-Centered Leadership**

"Doug Kirkpatrick's ideas on self-managed organizations grabbed the minds of the 2013 TEDxChico audience! He offered the type of challenge to old habits that brought people to ask themselves, 'Why not?' The future depends on people like Doug who intrigue us to increase business effectiveness by changing how we define people's roles."

—Laura Joplin

Speaker and Family Estate Representative
Author, **Love, Janis**

"Doug's first book was the fascinating story of a self-managing enterprise. His second is no story; it's a call to action with a whole new voice. *The No-Limits Enterprise* is dynamite!"

—Ken Everett

Author, **Designing the Networked Organization**
Cofounder, N2NHUB

"Make no mistake, even if you are a millennial, this landmark book will disrupt all your assumptions about managing your business, and most importantly, managing your life. You will never be the same again. Self-management is the new reality of business in the twenty-first century. And it is long overdue. This captivating new playbook of business will help you build the critical skills that will define the winners and losers of business, and life, going forward."

—Milton Pedraza

CEO, Luxury Institute

"Doug's work shows us that not only does self-management prove to make organizations more efficient, but also—and most importantly—that it makes the people within more happy, loyal, and valuable, which leads to greater amounts of meaningful, life-changing innovation. If you love the work you do, you will provide value to the world. Self-management just happens to be a great way to make people love their work, and this book explains both why and how."

—Paul Walker

Employee Experience Consultant, Zappos

"In his characteristic down-to-earth way, Doug Kirkpatrick presents a logical new narrative for switching from 'spirit-breaking control' to returning power and initiative back to the individual and collective. *The No-Limits Enterprise* is fueled by liberating human potential to focus on creating value for society at a critical time in human evolution. A must read for visionaries and operational pragmatists alike."

—Dawna Jones

Chief Provocateur, Provocateur Leadership Inc.

"Doug Kirkpatrick is today's prime global exponent of the art and science of self-management. The systematic techniques of self-management are perhaps the most influential innovation in business leadership in recent times. In his writing, Doug superbly exhibits the four crucial traits of any authentic practical teamwork. It is amazingly comprehensive, lucidly hands-on, exceptionally clear, and detailed with examples. In our current socio-political and economic-technological chaos, this focused approach is our essential compass. All is stringently based on the classical philosophies—effective at the foundations—of freedom of the will, accountability, character, and service genius. This is the book for our time!"

—Peter Koestenbaum

Author, The Inner Side of Greatness, A Philosophy for Leaders *and* The Vitality of Death

"This book is a must read for every leader—even if you cannot comprehend how an organization can be self-managed. Learn from a real expert who had firsthand experience starting and working at a company that implemented self-management. Amazing examples and principles are covered throughout the book. We all need to be prepared for the future."

—Ozlem Brooke Erol

Author, Speaker, and Consultant
Founder, Purposeful Business

"As an industrial engineer, growing up with a passion for never-ending improvement, I always felt the need to eliminate waste in the processes of the industrial-age companies I worked for. But as the knowledge age appeared, I realized that one form of waste—the waste of human talent—was still largely unaddressed. Doug Kirkpatrick's latest book that tackles self-management in the new age, was a revelation for me, providing the rationale and the means to ensure all human talents can realize their fullest potential. By driving out the waste embedded in management hierarchies, we can let uninterrupted work flow naturally toward creating value for customers, continuous innovation for our companies, and fulfilment for ourselves. This book is powerful in its elegance. It is uplifting in its promise. It will change companies and societies so we can confidently face the challenges of the knowledge age."

—Roger T. Burlton
President, Process Renewal Group

"This book is a must read. It reflects an emerging trend which is historically inevitable, and a scientific imperative: breaking free from out-of-date, nineteenth-century bureaucratic thinking for a dynamic twenty-first-century world. With case studies, checklists, and more, it is an enjoyable read. It will pose, for some, uncomfortable—but vital—questions which need to be answered if a company is to thrive."

—Nick Obolensky
CEO and Author, **Complex Adaptive Leadership**

"Doug Kirkpatrick has long been a guru to the world of self-managed organizations; and if that sounds like an oxymoron, you need to read his latest book! In it he makes a strong case for transforming traditional hierarchies—with their lack of agility, high turnover, soul-deadening strictures, and sheer waste—into fluid, dynamic networks of innovation, passion, and leadership. There is much more than evangelizing here; Doug helpfully provides the specific tools, templates, and practices that drive the transformation, along with plenty of stories to illustrate how it happens (or fails to happen) in real organizations. In the end, however, I was most struck by this powerful precept that captures the essence of self-management: 'Trust in the simplest of all human traits: the desire to create with dedication and love.'"

—Jocelyn Davis

Author, The Art of Quiet Influence *and* The Greats on Leadership

"*The No-Limits Enterprise* is a practical primer for business leaders who are truly serious about leading organizations that are smart, lean, nimble, and adaptable. Drawing upon his extensive firsthand knowledge and experience, Doug Kirkpatrick provides readers with a treasure trove of systems, tools, practices, checklists, templates, and case stories that they can immediately use to build organizations that are better designed to meet the increasing demands of a rapidly changing world."

—Rod Collins

Author, Wiki Management: A Revolutionary New Model for a Rapidly Changing and Collaborative World

"There are many wise voices out there criticizing traditional management and leadership practices. There are fewer who also can spell out clear and tangible alternatives, and even fewer who have practical experience in implementing radically different and better management models. Doug Kirkpatrick is one of them. With his firsthand experience from the amazing Morning Star journey, he addresses these important issues with an insight and authority that few can match. I have known Doug for many years and heard him speak on many occasions. His passion and knowledge shine brightly in this highly readable and recommendable book."

—Bjarte Bogsnes

Chairman, Beyond Budgeting Roundtable
Senior Advisor, Equinor

"If *Practical Wisdom* by Barry Schwartz and Kenneth Sharpe were to have a love child with *Orbiting the Giant Hairball* by Gordon MacKenzie, I believe the result would be Doug Kirkpatrick's *The No-Limits Enterprise*. This book combines critical insight and practical steps with a raw and honest reality: true creative human potential can only happen when people are allowed to openly express their passions in environments that don't crush them under a corporation's gravity. A true evolutionary leap in how businesses can develop resiliency, innovation, and competitive advantages based on self-management principles and solid business examples."

—Gary Keil, PhD

Board of Directors, Pharmacy Leadership and Educational Institute (PLEI) and The Leadership Institute for Development Education and Research (LiDER)

"A stimulating and much-needed book on new ways of organizing, with an up-to-date review of 'self-management' and the future of organizations. The book offers an overview of various strands of self-management, enabling organizations to move away from bureaucratic hierarchy and find their own way to self-management and what works for them. It contains principles, methodologies, tools, practices, stories, cases, challenges, examples, and transition advice to help them along the way. The backbone of this book is the author's experience of Morning Star, the famously self-managed tomato processing firm. It is obvious it has been written not from an academic perspective, but by someone who has lived it, breathed its benefits, and spoken with pure passion and belief for benefits that self-management brings and holds for a brighter future.

What organizations now require is the exact opposite of Max Weber's principles of dehumanized work and efficient bureaucracy. Today's challenges are so unpredictable, volatile, and complex that bureaucracies no longer work. We need to unlearn the past century, rehumanize work, and create workplaces where everyone has a voice. Over the centuries we have gradually shifted from total command, as in slavery, toward zero command, as in much of modern society (cities, communities, networks …). It is thus astounding that our companies, who are at the forefront of innovation and technology, are so backwards and mired in a command mentality when it comes to human organization, giving rise to our costly, unwieldy, and sometimes monstrous corporations. This book offers a clear way beyond and forward, not based on theory, but based on organizations, both small and large, that have already done it with great success."

—François Knuchel

Advisor, Next Stage Organizations and Living Systems

"The new business environment is too complex for traditional, command-and-control management which is why self-management is emerging as a better way to live and work. Nobody knows or understands this better than Doug Kirkpatrick who has been on the frontline of its development. Anybody looking for smarter and more humane ways to work, that dignify everyone involved, will find a treasure trove of ideas and experience in this book. It could not come at a better time."

—Margaret Heffernan

CEO and Author, Willful Blindness

"Doug's new book is a masterpiece: brilliantly conceived, beautifully written, poignantly humane, and remarkably practical. If you believe that employees are able to organize themselves on their own and do extraordinary work without the 'adult supervision' that so often constrains people in the workplace, you will love *The No-Limits Enterprise*. It shines a bright light on the promise and power to shape organizations in a way that produces amazing business success, while elevating the humanity and the performance of every person in the organization."

—Les Landes

President, Landes & Associates

Author, Getting to the Heart of Employee Engagement

"In *The No-Limits Enterprise*, Doug Kirkpatrick shows us that the future is now. This book takes a smart, provocative look at how the worlds of work and human development are becoming synonymous. Best of all, *The No-Limits Enterprise* provides us with a roadmap for creating a self-managed organization—one in which innovation, self-accountability, and empowerment drive superior business performance."

—Claudette Rowley

Founder, Cultural Brilliance
Author, Cultural Brilliance: The DNA of Organizational Excellence

"Doug Kirkpatrick's pioneering spirit and depth of firsthand experience offer a compelling view of how organizations must radically change to adapt to today's reality. *The No-Limits Enterprise* delivers a concise reference for the burgeoning self-managed organization."

—Jose Leal

Cofounder, Radical

"In an era where new ways of working are on the rise, it is a comfort to know that Doug Kirkpatrick has trodden the path before us. With almost three decades of experience working and advising self-managed organization, Doug has a wealth of knowledge about how to implement revolutionary ways of working. Listen to what he has to say and follow his advice. You're liable to build a company where people are free to do the best work of their lives."

—Robin P. Zander

Founder, Zander Media
Executive Director, Responsive Conference

"For many people, discussing a self-managing organization still feels a bit like talking about a unicorn: it sounds amazing, but feels impossibly fictional. With *The No-Limits Enterprise*, in his disarmingly straightforward, easy-to-follow, no-BS way, Doug Kirkpatrick shows clearly that organizational self-management is not only real, it's a vastly superior way of working."

—Josh Allan Dykstra

Author, Igniting the Invisible Tribe: Designing An Organization That Doesn't Suck

"Doug Kirkpatrick animates the concept of self-management and brings to life the surprising benefits, colorful history, and sheer urgency for why people at all levels in the workplace matter and possess limitless power. This book challenged me, caused me to ponder, and ultimately inspired me to be a better leader."

—Annie Snowbarger

Founding Member, HPWP Group

"Doug Kirkpatrick dares us to consider a different path to the future for our organizations. Through numerous examples with supporting research, he builds a provocative argument for unleashing the full potential of our talent by creating structures that lift rather than constrain and trust our people to show the way."

—Debra France, EdD

W.L. Gore & Associates

"I've spent most of my adult life guiding organizations coping with rapid and transformational change. It's hard, complex work, and often feels hopeless. Doug Kirkpatrick has spent his life turning a vision of the power and simplicity of self-management principles into an organizational reality. It's refreshing to see an approach that works and produces incredible benefits for everyone from the C-suite to the front line. This book is full of stories that prove the power of self-management; more importantly, the storytellers demonstrate with ultimate clarity how you can do it too. Doug is a passionate, committed trail guide on the pathway to the future of work."

—James Ware, PhD

Author, Making Meetings Matter: How Smart Leaders Orchestrate Powerful Conversations in the Digital Age

"As more and more organizations begin to focus on what 'the future of work' means for them, they should also be thinking about what the future workplace looks like. Doug offers a compelling blueprint for transforming workplace cultures through self-management principles. Full of examples, tools, checklists, and other useful resources, this book is both inspiring and practical. Those who want to create flat, high-achieving workplace cultures will find this book compelling."

—Tony Bingham

President and CEO, Association for Talent Development

"Bureaucracy and top-down business tyranny have been obsolete for a very long time. Self-management is an empowering and exponentially more profitable business framework. In *The No-Limits Enterprise*, Kirkpatrick eloquently debunks all the detractors who claim 'it will never work here' and offers a practical roadmap that can be followed by any company. Kirkpatrick knows. He has been living and breathing self-management for more than three decades. Beware—this may be the most liberating business book you will ever read. We need it now, more than ever. Liberate yourself!"

—Achim Nowak

Author, Business Thinker, Mastermind Convener, and C-Suite Success Coach

THE NO-LIMITS ENTERPRISE

DOUG KIRKPATRICK

THE NO-LIMITS ENTERPRISE

ORGANIZATIONAL SELF-MANAGEMENT IN THE NEW WORLD OF WORK

Forbes | Books

Published by ForbesBooks, Charleston, South Carolina.
Member of Advantage Media Group.

ForbesBooks is a registered trademark, and the ForbesBooks colophon is a trademark of Forbes Media, LLC.

Printed in the United States of America.

10 9 8 7 6 5 4 3 2 1

ISBN: 978-1-946633-27-9 (hardcover)
ISBN: 979-8-88750-514-5 (paperback)
LCCN: 2019934682

Book design by Megan Elger.

This publication is designed to provide accurate and authoritative information in regard to the subject matter covered. It is sold with the understanding that the publisher is not engaged in rendering legal, accounting, or other professional services. If legal advice or other expert assistance is required, the services of a competent professional person should be sought.

Advantage Media Group is proud to be a part of the Tree Neutral® program. Tree Neutral offsets the number of trees consumed in the production and printing of this book by taking proactive steps such as planting trees in direct proportion to the number of trees used to print books. To learn more about Tree Neutral, please visit **www.treeneutral.com**.

Since 1917, the Forbes mission has remained constant. Global Champions of Entrepreneurial Capitalism. ForbesBooks exists to further that aim by bringing the Stories, Passion, and Knowledge of top thought leaders to the forefront. ForbesBooks brings you The Best in Business. To be considered for publication, please visit **www.forbesbooks.com**.

To my dear friend and mentor, Peter Koestenbaum, PhD,
and to the leaders he has challenged into greatness.
We all stand on the shoulders of giants.

TABLE OF CONTENTS

ACKNOWLEDGMENTS

This book reflects the hard-won wisdom and keen insight of several very important people, and draws energy from several valuable communities.

First, I wish to thank my friend and mentor Peter Koestenbaum, PhD, author of *Leadership: The Inner Side of Greatness,* and founder of the Koestenbaum Institute. After a childhood spent partly in Hitler's Germany, he embarked on a lifetime of acclaimed teaching, writing, and consulting. He remains a tireless advocate for organizational self-management and for the respect of the depth and complexity of the leadership mind.

Thanks go out to inspiring people who freely shared their crucial insights and wisdom over the last few years: Brian Rocha of Fresh Fill; Stephenie Gloden of the Apollo Group; Lori Kane, EdD of Collective Self; Buurtzorg founder, Jos de Blok; Haier Group founder, Zhang Ruimin; Debra France, EdD of W.L. Gore & Associates; Chuck Blakeman of the Crankset Group; Traci Fenton and Miranda Ash of WorldBlu; Tony Bingham of the Association for Talent Development; Gary Hamel and Michele Zanini of the Management Information eXchange; Tom Thomison of Encode. org; Michael Pacanowsky at the Center for Innovative Cultures; Paul Green, Jr. at the University of Texas; John Thompson at People-Centric Organizations; Milton Pedraza at the Luxury Institute; Dawna Jones of InSight Out Consulting; Matt Perez of Nearsoft; Scott Heiferman of Meetup; Mario Kaphan of Vagas; author and thought leader, Margaret Heffernan; Robin Zander of Responsive; Jose Leal of Radical; Susan Basterfield of Enspiral; Alanna Irving of

Open Source Collective; Josh Allan Dykstra of Helios; Ken Everett of N2NHUB; Pim de Morree and Joost Minnaar of Corporate Rebels; Management 3.0 evangelist, Jurgen Appelo; Evan Leybourn of Business Agility Institute; Ben Roberts of The Conversation Collaborative; Achim Nowak of BRILLIANT BEST; Ruth Simone of Luminare Coaching; Daniel Mezick of New Technology Solutions, Inc.; thought leader, Jon Husband; COS-Journal founder, Maria Spindler; Keith McCandless of Liberating Structures; Jaipur Rugs founder Nand Kishore Chaudhary; and Ricardo Semler of Semco Partners and the author of *Maverick* and *The Seven-Day Weekend*. I am profoundly grateful for each and every conversation with these inspirers and many, many others too numerous to list here.

My former professional colleague at NuFocus Strategic Group, Suzanne Daigle, is an inspiring and tireless encourager and advocate for the self-managed, purpose-driven, and inclusive workplaces of the rising generation.

Roger Burlton and Sasha Aganova of the Process Renewal Group are visionary practitioners of superior business process execution and generously provide platforms, personal energy, and content to make the case for organizational self-management.

Appreciation to my high school debate coach and wonderful friend, Susan Rowberry Davis, who gave me the ability to ask good questions and take good notes, which is frequently helpful when writing a book.

Much-deserved thanks go to friends and colleagues in multiple organizations and communities from which I draw energy and passion: Great Work Cultures, Association for Talent Development, Center for Innovative Cultures, Rework CEO, Work Revolution, Responsive, People-Centric Organizations, Radical, Business

Agility Institute, and many others. Their work is inspiring and world changing.

Deep appreciation goes to Chris J. Rufer, entrepreneur extraordinaire and founder of The Morning Star Company, from whom I learned most of what I know about business. He insisted that our early leadership team read a newly published book, *In Search of Excellence*, by Tom Peters and Robert H. Waterman. My response to that book crystallized a lifelong curiosity about high-performing organizations and how they work.

Finally, I wish to thank my friends and colleagues at The Morning Star Company, past and present, for bravely manifesting self-management each and every day at work. They are true pioneers.

FOREWORD

We all routinely engage in self-management, but we seldom notice. We decide what to pay attention to and what books to read. We decide where to live, what to wear, and what to eat. We decide when to work, when to play, when to speak, and when to listen.

We also decide what kind of work we prefer to do. And where to best find and then do that kind of work each day. We decide on who we wish to associate with. To do this successfully, we must first confirm that the other party wants the association as well. We must confirm that they are willing and able; we must obtain their consent.

In his previous book, *Beyond Empowerment*, Doug clearly defines self-management as applied to organizations: "Organizational self-management is the philosophy of individuals freely and autonomously performing the traditional functions of management (planning, organizing, coordinating, staffing, directing, controlling) guided by principles and without mechanistic hierarchy or arbitrary, unilateral command authority over others."

So, what you are getting into with this book is the application of a profoundly powerful philosophy, one that has the potential to change your work and your life. With this book Doug does a great job of both describing it and teaching you how to apply it. In Part II, Doug offers you a clear and practical implementation roadmap, with several tools to help orient and guide you along the way. What you're getting into here is an immensely practical book.

And a timely one. There's an unstoppable force that is driving the philosophy of organizational self-management forward. And that force is the relentless pace of change, driven by technology. Nowhere is this more apparent than in the new world of work.

Organizations that cannot move quickly are discovering that they simply cannot compete. The ability to sense and respond, especially at scale, is now essential to survival. Organizations that are using self-management are thriving precisely because they are more efficient, more aware, more adaptive, and more opportunistic than those who are not.

It is no coincidence that many of the enterprises who have successfully embraced self-management are often organizations that sell software as a product or a service. These contemporary companies understand the relentless pace of change, and how to apply more organizational self-management when the pace of change speeds up.

This trend is a large one, and it's just getting underway. This new book from Doug is an important one that helps define the entire domain. *The No-Limits Enterprise* is your tutorial and reference guide on the principles and step-by-step implementation of organizational self-management.

I believe that Doug's book is sure to be widely cited and stand the test of time. I hope you enjoy it.

—Daniel Mezick
www.DanielMezick.com
Author, *The Culture Game, The OpenSpace Agility Handbook,* and *Inviting Leadership: Invitation-Based Change™ in the New World of Work*
Guilford, Connecticut
January 22, 2019

LIFE IS A CONCERT
(OR IT SHOULD BE)

The simplest principles produce the most
powerful and astonishing effects.

—THOMAS DICK, NINETEENTH-CENTURY MINISTER,

ASTRONOMER, AND PHILOSOPHER

SOME PEOPLE ARE LUCKY: they experience a seminal moment in life when what they believe, aspire to, dream, and practice come together in a single crystallizing experience. For me, one of those moments came a few years back, taking in a Leahy concert.

Leahy, the band, consists of eight of the eleven Leahy siblings raised in rural Ontario. Leahy, the phenomenon, is a dynamic, explosive, pulsating assemblage of the most skilled and talented musician-dancers most of us will ever see. How these men and women do what they do is nothing short of wondrous. Most anyone—fan of Irish ancestral music or not—would be astounded by the sheer synchronicity of a Leahy performance and the level of excellence the family of artists achieves. The night I attended their concert, I watched the band members come together, move apart, and hand off the spotlight to one another, all while working in perfect concert and sustaining a pitch, energy, and intensity that never flagged. There was no apparent leader; in the continual flow of the hand-offs, the leader of the moment was whoever was *needed* to be the leader. There were no subordinate musicians or dancers. All were essential to the success of the performance. A band member would at times be highlighted; at other moments, he or she would step back to cheer others on.

Leahy is a family and a band, but as I watched that night with so many others in the audience, Leahy became what the siblings themselves laughingly admit Leahy is: a *verb*. That's because, in its performances, Leahy is soaring toward perfection. Leahy band members are free to pursue their work with passion and joy, each taking their own achievement to higher and higher levels, to the benefit of the whole.

And, as band members explained in ongoing patter during the course of their performance, Leahy is also a *noun*: it is an organization that has pinned mission, strategy, and process behind its art. Leahy siblings are colleagues who freely and fervently believe in the Leahy mission, do everything they can to support the strategy, and enthusiastically work the process. Collaboration undergirds everything; control from any one source would extinguish the joy. Each player's virtuosity and execution is cheered on toward perfection, propelling Leahy, as an entity, to higher and higher planes.

Even during a single evening's concert, it was apparent that the familial connection among the siblings is at times mentorship, too. Adjustments during the performance are accepted by all; they only improve the result. In the end, a vigorous, constantly shifting form of teamwork morphs into sublime synchronicity right before the audience.

Never had I witnessed the true meaning of *working in concert*, as I did the night I took in a Leahy performance.

Afterward, I thought about what this transcendent group of musicians could teach us all about passion, equality, and the joy of working in such a way that each of us leads, innovates, and performs to our highest levels. Within the space of two hours or so, I witnessed a clear, real-life demonstration of simple principles (passion, equality, and the joy of working) producing magnificent complexity (astounding talent and orchestration across countless levels).

> *I witnessed a clear, real-life demonstration of simple principles (passion, equality, and the joy of working) producing magnificent complexity.*

In the end, the elation I experienced that evening served to bolster my belief in my own life's work—that of helping business enterprises succeed by relinquishing age-old entrenched beliefs and moving toward two simple and basic life-affirming principles:

- One, that people work best when they are happy and passionate about their work.

- Two, that they produce and innovate on their highest levels when they are not coerced to work but are simply expected to keep the commitments that they freely make to their colleagues and their organization.

Such simple tenets; and they are by no means new. The codes of commitment and non-coercion have served as the underlayment of legal systems and ethics throughout history. When you think about it, our Founding Fathers employed these very tenets to form the American system of government. In every way they could foresee, the earliest leaders of our nation instituted systems of checks and balances to protect human freedoms. They did this so that people could pursue their inalienable rights to life, liberty, and the pursuit of happiness as they saw fit; so that they could manage their own destiny. In the end, coercive rule over the colonists did indeed result in the downfall of British control over the colonies, and the great American experiment in self-determination was launched.

Clearly, bringing passion, heart, and humanity to law, governing, and the management of daily life in general is not just a "nice" thing to do. The chances of the entire machine of civilization succeeding are greater when the human beings needed to turn the wheels are free to operate at their highest levels, and when we reduce or eliminate the degree to which any one group or faction can exercise authority over others. Life, as a whole, works better when we all invest in a state of freedom, autonomy, and goodwill.

And so it is in the workplace: people who are encouraged to innovate, lead, and perform, perform best. And yet, Gallup's *State of the American Workplace* publication reports that only 33 percent of American workers are engaged at work, with 16 percent "actively disengaged"—costing the US $483 billion to $605 billion each year in lost productivity.[1]

People who are encouraged to innovate, lead, and perform, perform best.

The fact of the matter is, companies simply can't afford to have their employees disengaged

---

1   "State of the American Workplace," Gallup, 2017, https://www.gallup.com/ workplace/238085/state-american-workplace-report-2017.aspx?g_source=link_ NEWSV9&g_medium=TOPIC&g_campaign=item_&g_content=State%2520of%2520the%25 20American%2520Workplace.

and hating—or at least not loving—their jobs. Traditional management is broken. We need a new, twenty-first-century approach to management that will galvanize the minds—and hearts—of people giving so much of their lives to organizations.

At its core, then, is success in the workplace all about *love*? Chris Rufer, the founder of The Morning Star Company, put this question to me years ago in a leadership meeting that took place prior to launching the company. California-based Morning Star has since become the world's leading processor of tomato products. No coincidence, it is also a leading model of a wholly self-managed enterprise. I was a member of that company's launch team.

While constructing the company's first factory in Los Banos in 1990, Rufer became convinced that self-management was the right operating system for his organization. As a trucking company owner in the 1970s and early 1980s, he had noticed how, despite ever-present layers of management, the factories where he delivered his loads were mostly inefficient and poorly run. He was convinced that pointless bureaucracy was behind much of the ineffectiveness and disengagement that he saw. Rufer decided that Morning Star should have *no* levels of management. Just as they did in the outside world, the company's colleagues (who formerly would have been called "employees") would manage *themselves* as they moved through negotiated commitments to their colleagues and the enterprise as a whole. His burning question, which reverberated through the years, was, "What's work got to do with love?"

That day (after we realized he wasn't joking), we hashed around the notion of love in the workplace and blurted out some thoughts, but never answered his question to his satisfaction. Recently, however, I came across what constitutes the best response yet, courtesy of Kahlil Gibran: "Work is love made visible." Gibran went on to add,

"And if you cannot work with love but only with distaste, it is better that you should leave your work and sit at the gate of the temple and take alms of those who work with joy."

The second part of the quote may be a bit harsh but, when you think about it, work *is* love made visible. By creating value for others, we are expressing our generosity to our fellow human beings. After all, we can't see a paycheck as our only motivation and satisfaction for constructing a safer car, building a better pacemaker, or solving the mysteries of the universe. People who love what they do are giving to others *through* what they do. What's more, by reintegrating humanity back into the workplace, it turns out that we go home and spread the love throughout the rest of our lives, as well.

A couple of years back, Stephenie Gloden, an IT and customer service business unit leader at the University of Phoenix, discovered my first book, *Beyond Empowerment: The Age of the Self-Managed Organization*,[2] and decided that the principles would work well at her company. According to Stephenie, her fifty-person unit had been experiencing problems with peer accountability and trust; as a result, the group was having trouble functioning in the business's new agile structure. Although the company had taken the position of empowering its employees to be more autonomous, its hierarchical chain of command was still sending a different message. Stephenie's team members were hesitant to circumvent the management structure, and she had been searching for help.

In a 2017 podcast interview, Stephenie recalled: "Doug asked a question in the book that really hit home with us. When you're on your own in your personal life and you are buying a home—a huge decision to make—who do you ask permission to do that? You

---

2   Doug Kirkpatrick, *Beyond Empowerment: The Age of the Self-Managed Organization* (Rochester: Jetlaunch, 2017).

don't! You might consult or do your homework, but you are making that very large decision on your own. So, why is it when you walk through the doors of your organization, you can't make a similar large decision?"

Twelve months after her team read and discussed *Beyond Empowerment*, her unit had implemented self-management successfully and its roadblocks were gone. The unit members then uncovered a curious byproduct of the exercise: the principles had not only proved tremendously helpful to the team members' work lives, but all of the members found that, because the principles were so fundamental, they had been inadvertently incorporating the principles into every aspect of life outside of the workplace—civic, community, family, and faith.

"It absolutely changed how we see people and has helped each of us to grow as a human being," Stephenie explained. One-to-one accountability in the workplace, she said, helped everyone to *fundamentally* care about others and "see the other person sitting beside me." This was a vastly different approach than in a hierarchically structured organization where workers look to their higher-ups to manage employee relationships and intervene between individuals and groups when problems occur.

Stephenie's story also brings to mind that of Buurtzorg, a highly prosperous Netherlands-based health care company, entirely self-managed. Visionary founder Jos de Blok and the people of Buurtzorg believe deeply in autonomy and self-management and have created a system in which decision-making power comes from the employees rather than from bosses, with a devolved structure that has eliminated middle management. Buurtzorg's nine thousand home health care nurses work remotely and travel to client patients to deliver care, making decisions as needed because they are closest to the patients.

The health care workers are employed by the company, but are treated as independent professionals. Buurtzorg is an outstanding example of self-management in action.

One would think that in an era of enterprises launched by young entrepreneurs and increasingly populated by millennial workers, organizations would be "flattening" their hierarchies at a record pace. After all, it has been widely reported that millennials, especially, do not function well within conventionally hierarchical organizations. In fact, when they cannot self-manage and innovate, these young people tend to flee. With two millennial daughters, I have firsthand knowledge of this phenomenon. One daughter worked for a technology publication with a progressive twenty-first-century image—surely a workplace of the future yet, as it turned out, not so much. The company was still structured as any 1800s organization would have been. My other daughter was employed by a well-known Los Angeles-based nonprofit. There were only ten employees in her office, yet there were four layers of management to penetrate before anything could get done.

Organizations may sell themselves as young, entrepreneurial, and futuristic, while still operating as archaic models of the Industrial Age. But increasingly, millennials are making it clear that, unlike the baby boomers before them, they will not pay their dues by doing trivial work for years, slaving away nights and weekends to prove themselves. Today, media outlets everywhere report that millennials are disrupting professions and businesses such as health care and banking. These verticals are indeed struggling to attract, onboard, and retain the incoming workforce. The campaign has become global as companies everywhere are finally modifying age-old organizational paradigms to keep millennials in-house. (I recently spoke with business leaders in Dubai, for instance, who are grappling with the same issues we are in the US.)

The world has changed a good deal since my first day of school when the teacher handed out crayons and an outline of a buffalo and told her students to color the buffalo brown. That day, I wanted to use two different colors to create my own special buffalo—and consequently flunked the opening assignment of my academic career. I learned then that being creative, innovative, and passionate about work was not valued; doing what I was told to do, was.

Not surprisingly, as an adult I became fascinated by the tension between *organizational freedom* and *accountability*. (How can we be free to innovate within an organization? To whom do we owe accountability for our work, responsibilities, and what we ultimately achieve in the workplace?) I was privileged to serve as the first financial controller for The Morning Star Company, where Chris Rufer introduced the core principles of self-management. At Morning Star, I learned that organizational self-management is real, it works, and it drives superior business performance.

In 2008, I helped establish the Morning Star Self-Management Institute, with the mission of making organizational self-management principles tangible and viable through effective education, tools, and practices. A serious but life-affirming car accident in 2013 only served to renew my commitment to share a vision of a better future state for workplaces all around the world and, instead of sidelining me, it galvanized my determination to see the twenty-first-century enterprise reborn.

Today, as a partner in the full-spectrum international consulting firm, NuFocus Strategic Group, I speak and consult on self-management throughout North America and around the world. And I share the message of organizational innovation through my books, TEDx talks, articles, and posts. Organizational innovation is my personal calling, and I also engage with Great Work Cultures,[3] The Work Revolution,[4] the Center for Innovative Cultures,[5] and other groups and communities to co-create the organizations of the future.

Here, within these pages, you can begin your own journey toward a twenty-first-century enterprise with limitless potential for growth. With this book, you will gain a true understanding of the immeasurable power of your own workplace and workforce. Inside, you will learn:

- Why the domestic and global breakdown of bureaucracy means the future of the workplace is here *right now.*

- How the principles of self-management, fundamental to life itself, give self-management *limitless power* networked across the workplace. Innovation, leadership, and passion are everywhere, propelling the enterprise to unbounded heights.

- Why "managing" others in the workplace is obsolete and, ultimately, self-defeating on so many levels.

- Why, right now, your own company is paying a massive "management tax," and how you can use those funds to invest in immediate growth, instead.

- How modern drivers of self-management are transforming traditional hierarchies into networks for various enterprises—and that can include yours.

- How to rigorously self-assess for success, corporately and personally, before embarking on enterprise transformation.

---

3   greatworkcultures.org
4   workrevolution.org
5   innovativecultures.org

- How to think through and skillfully manage considerations and implications for self-management prior to implementation.

- How to make a powerful case for a self-management transformation to others across the enterprise.

- How to use real-world self-management models and proven best practices for your own enterprise transformation roadmap to ensure success.

Yes, the world has changed quite a bit since we were expected to color with a single crayon, stay within the lines, and not ask questions. Today, our fast-moving, ever-expanding world demands engaged, innovative, and self-directed leaders. These are leaders who may emerge from any corner of an organization. These are leaders who will fearlessly set about to create work environments where everyone strives in concert, uncoerced, and committed to the passionate pursuit of excellence within an enterprise positioned for unlimited success. *Any* business can transform itself into a No-Limits Enterprise in which every individual is free to innovate and forge new paths to the immense benefit of all. These challenges do not demand complex layers of management; they demand the ability to jettison ancient layers of control, and trust

Any business can transform itself into a No-Limits Enterprise in which every individual is free to innovate and forge new paths to the immense benefit of all. These challenges do not demand complex layers of management; they demand the ability to jettison ancient layers of control, and trust in the simplest of all human traits: the desire to create with dedication and love.

in the simplest of all human traits: the desire to create with dedication and love.

—**Doug Kirkpatrick**, San Francisco, California, 2019

PART I

THE PROMISE OF SELF-MANAGEMENT

Simple, clear purpose and principles give rise to complex intelligent behavior. Complex rules and regulations give rise to simple stupid behavior.

—**DEE W. HOCK, FOUNDER OF VISA**

CHAPTER 1

THE BREAKDOWN OF
BUREAUCRACY

*I can say, without the slightest hesitation, that the science of
handling pig-iron is so great that the man who is physically
able to handle pig-iron and is sufficiently phlegmatic
and stupid to choose this for his occupation is rarely able
to comprehend the science of handling pig-iron.*

—**FREDERICK WINSLOW TAYLOR, AMERICAN INVENTOR,
ENGINEER, AND FATHER OF SCIENTIFIC MANAGEMENT**

IN THE SPRING OF 1990, in a tiny farmhouse on the outskirts of Los Banos, California, inside a kitchen "conference room," trucking entrepreneur Chris Rufer was planning the construction of a tomato processing plant and founding what would become a fully networked, nonhierarchical manufacturing enterprise: The Morning Star Company. Not coincidentally, the now-three California Morning Star processing facilities are the biggest individual plants in the industry and together comprise the largest tomato processing company in the world. Yet, back in 1990, as tomato seeds were already sprouting and Rufer and his launch team were focusing on getting the new factory up and running, he realized that a successful startup in the industry would require a wholly new kind of edge. After all, stakeholder obligations, personal guarantees, and relocated workers had ramped up the stakes.

But Rufer was also thinking about something else. With the benefit of an MBA (along with years of self-study in philosophy), he was considering the persistent nineteenth-century model of bureaucracy in the workplace, and how it hindered the success of enterprises large and small. In his previous incarnation as the founder of the Morning Star one-rig trucking outfit, he had not only put himself through college, he had noted time and again that the factories where he delivered his loads—prime examples of bureaucratic management—were often poorly run.

Bureaucracy in the workplace, Rufer decided, stifled human freedom, creativity, innovation, and collaboration. He saw that, in the process, it obstructed the pursuit of excellence and, counter to its original intention, prevented enterprises from succeeding as they should. Rufer had long been intrigued by the relationship of philosophy, human principles, and management practices in the workplace. He had read extensively on these subjects. He came to believe that people worked best when they were free to manage themselves at work just as they managed themselves in their daily lives. Moreover, he was convinced that those who were free to learn to manage themselves skillfully and confidently were generally happiest and most successful in life. People, he decided, were *fundamentally* self-managed beings, and functioned best that way. He concluded that a self-managed enterprise was therefore the best possible model for the ultimate success of workers and enterprises alike.

Rufer's new tomato processing plant, christened Morning Star like its trucking company predecessor, would be constructed not just of steel and brick; it would rely upon a philosophy-and-principles-based "natural process" framework and would test his theory. In the totally flat (nonhierarchical) Morning Star work environment, there would be no managers of others and no acceptable coercion. The organization's colleagues would succeed by way of rock-solid commitments to one another as they moved through their daily work processes.

As it turned out, both the Morning Star workers and their organization succeeded brilliantly. According to business process authority Roger T. Burlton writing in his book *Business Process Management: Profiting from Process* (2001), "Morning Star is the best example I've seen of a mature, process-managed company. Nowhere else have I witnessed or even heard of a company that's so driven to manage its relationships in such a natural way—totally process-empowered and a great place to work."

In the years since Burlton's enthusiastic assessment of Morning Star, self-managed enterprises have emerged across the globe. Some are wholly flat, while others are better categorized as models for the workplace of the future, offering their own versions of organizing. These are often termed "cracies" such as *holacracy* (as in the online shoe retailer Zappos's circular, self-organizing teams). Yet, no matter which form of future-looking organization a company leader comes to embrace, beforehand each comes to the realization that bureaucracy does not work well either for twenty-first-century enterprises or the human beings at work within them. At least, not in the world as we know it today, and certainly not in the world we are soon to know.

Broken Bureaucracy

The fact of the matter is: the unwieldy, ineffective, bureaucratic, and hierarchical workplace model in which most people uncomfortably spend more than half their waking lives is irretrievably broken. Each year, massive sums of money and an astounding amount of company time are spent dealing solely with the management issues pertaining to production, sales, competitive edge, and strategic retooling—not on the initiatives themselves. These expenditures do not even take into account the time and money dedicated to human resources management issues, which encompass recruiting, hiring, onboarding, retention, engagement, workplace toxicity, lack of diversity, firing, outplacement, morale, harassment issues, and more.

As Gallup reports, 67 percent of the US workplace are disengaged from their organization at any given time, and 16 percent of workers are actively disengaged from the organization. One can imagine myriad forms of active disengagement, including unsafe work practices, gossip, harassment, drug use, inappropriate use of social media, absenteeism, and even sabotage. With the hard-dol-

As Gallup reports, 67 percent of the US workplace are disengaged from their organization at any given time, and 16 percent of workers are actively disengaged from the organization.

lar cost of such disengagement pegged at around a half-*trillion* dollars in lost production each year, the report points to nothing short of a management crisis that is having serious and lasting repercussions on the global economy.[6]

A Workplace Without Bureaucracy

So, what would the workplace be like if the people within it worked on activities that made them happy and allowed them to enjoy productive and satisfying working relationships with their peers, uncoerced to "perform," and creating value and delight for other human beings? Is it a Utopian dream to believe that people at work can be respectful of one another's time, compassion, and energy as they also generously contribute to society and the rest of humanity?

What if I told you that the aforementioned scenario would enable a business—*your* business—to focus 100 percent of its energy and attention on balancing the needs of all its stakeholders while delivering the best possible value in products and services to its customers? After all, the real-world definition of *profit* is "to create more value than you consume."

If the win-win-win for people, business, and society that I present sounds impossible to you, then you should know that right now, in more and more locations around the world, forward-thinking leaders like Chris Rufer are reaping the benefits of self-management, and you can, too. To get there, you will need to see the workplace and your company's potential in a whole new light, and you will also need to release long-held assumptions and beliefs that have not served you or your fellow business leaders for decades, possibly a

---

6   "State of the American Workplace," Gallup, 2017, https://www.gallup.com/workplace/238085/state-american-workplace-report-2017.aspx?g_source=link_NEWSV9&g_medium=TOPIC&g_campaign=item_&g_content=State%2520of%2520the%2520American%2520Workplace.

century. Right now, whether you know it or not, you and your business-leader brethren are mired in a nineteenth-century Industrial Age model of bureaucratic organizational hierarchy that is tottering under decaying layers of management. That management detritus has not been clearheadedly assessed for its true impact on the workplace and its people, your business and its profit potential, possibly *ever*.

It's time to take a good hard look at bureaucracy in the workplace and understand precisely why it no longer works.

Nineteenth-Century Bureaucracy in a Twenty-First-Century World

As the Industrial Age dawned in the late eighteenth century, business leaders everywhere began to look to existing organizational models to ramp up production and supply the goods and services needed by the masses. Not surprisingly, they quickly determined that the military offered the best (and, frankly, the only) organizational model for recruiting, mobilizing, training, organizing, and managing the huge cohorts of workers, unskilled and otherwise, that would be needed to produce vast quantities of products large and small. For a nation struggling to build a transcontinental railroad with only Morse code, telegraphs, and the Pony Express for information flow, bureaucracy was not just the best choice for decision-makers of the time, it was the *only* choice.

Product and service needs were rapidly expanding. Businesses required legions of workers to keep up with demand, and they needed to keep their workers producing at full tilt or suffer the competitive consequences. Management soon became the oil that greased the gears. Workers were the cogs that drove those gears and required the oil.

Frederick W. Taylor (contributor of the quotation that opened this chapter) surfaced as a leading voice of nineteenth-century management practices, setting the bars of bureaucracy in business for more than a century to come. Hailed as the father of scientific management, he believed in moving control *away* from workers (who had up to that time been determining the best ways to approach their tasks), to managers trained to oversee them. He maintained that for greatest efficiency in the new world of mass production, managers were best qualified to handle the intelligent planning work that the manual laborers would then execute as specified and communicated to them. Not long after, resentment in the workplace became an additionally compelling challenge for management. Worker rebellions and strikes became more commonplace. To meet the new management challenges, additional layers of managers of various kinds were added.

Over the next century, bureaucracy in the business world would go on to spawn layer after layer of command-and-control management through which information would trickle down to workers, but which would rarely flow in the reverse direction. Bosses would view their workers as expendable human "resources" or "manhours"—and management and its practices would mushroom to handle whole constellations of employee issues related to repression and resentment.

Repression or not, in the business world of the nineteenth century—an era of linear working processes that often required limited brainpower—having bosses, supervisors, managers, and submanagers with information cascading down through the ranks, military style, may have made a certain amount of sense. After all, communication systems were primitive; how else would workers have access to actionable information in anything that approached real time? In most facets of life, people relied on an information flow that came from decision-makers at the top, filtering down to the people doing the work.

Today, however, the concept of bureaucratic management is rife with challenges not only for the business world, but inside the military environments for which it was designed. For some time, the media has reported that the armed services are transitioning to self-managed models in select areas. Certain ranks and processes may persist, but whole divisions and entities, such as Navy SEAL teams and aircraft carrier flight-deck operations, are largely if not completely self-managed, as are the military's Blue Angels and Thunderbirds, flying in formation at 400-plus mph.

Conversely, it's no secret that throughout much of history, resentment and frustration with power and bureaucracy has at times manifested within armed service ranks as "fragging." During the Vietnam conflict, for instance, as commanding officers wielded absolute power and troops could not bear up under the strain, soldiers were known to have misdirected a grenade here or there in the direction of particularly oppressive officers. It seems that even those in the military don't cotton to unnecessary coercion when they are capable of managing themselves and the skills they have honed.

Lazy and Stupid vs. Working with Purpose

A quick review of Theory X and Theory Y, contrasting theories espoused in the late 1950s by Douglas McGregor at the MIT School of Management, makes the reasons for coercion resentment abundantly clear:

> **Theory X** (describing bureaucratic management thinking) assumes that rank-and-file employees have little ambition, will shirk work and responsibility if left unmanaged, and

are driven only by pursuit of their own goals. It supposes that these individuals seek to work for a living wage, are generally lazy, not inherently intelligent, and respond best to a reward/reprimand style of hands-on management.

Theory Y, on the other hand, assumes that most people work for personal satisfaction above income, want to enjoy their work, and are internally motivated to achieve for their organization. Such employees are considered valuable assets to a business concern and, beyond that, can actually drive the success of the company. Theory Y workers consider themselves responsible for their output, do not need to be managed by others to achieve it, and seek to create high quality products and services for their organizations.

A perfect example of a Theory Y organization in twenty-first-century practice is the near-flat W.L. Gore and Associates (makers of Gore-Tex fabrics, medical devices, and more), often dubbed the most innovative company in America. Via its self-managed associates, W.L. Gore is known for delivering outstanding results to customers and consumers, and for being a pioneer in espousing and implementing concepts that have made it an icon in workplace freedom. Year after year, W.L. Gore routinely ranks in the top tier of *Fortune* magazine's "100 Best Companies to Work For" while exceeding $3 billion in revenue annually.

On the other hand, a serious drawback of Theory X is the fact that, to a customer, the company is the individual in that organization who is interfacing with him. Anyone who has ever spent a couple of frustrating hours on the phone with a cable TV company representative knows what it feels like to be on the receiving end of a very long command-and-control chain. Neither customer nor employee emerges from such an interaction with good feelings about the conglomerate behind the curtain. But there can be even graver consequences for Theory X-modeled organizations that breed dysfunction. The most serious consequence is the breakdown of the organization's bureaucratic structure itself, often going unheeded until catastrophe strikes.

When Bureaucracy Breaks Down

While there have been countless incidences of bureaucratic business breakdowns in modern times, one of the most notable must be Union Carbide Corporation's December 1984 Bhopal Disaster, in which the death toll from a chemical gas leak was estimated by some sources to have hit 16,000 in the weeks, months, and years after the tragic incident. It has never been determined whether the leak itself was due to domino-like breakdowns of responsibility along chains of command (starting with then-UCC chairman and CEO Warren Anderson), or whether a disgruntled employee was guilty of sabotage. Still, it remains undisputed that widespread bureaucratic breakdown throughout the organization played a decisive role in the disaster.

Bureaucratic breakdowns are not always as transparent as in the Union Carbide disaster, for they are often insidious, even if pervasive. The causes of such breakdowns, however, usually hearken back to company workers who spend the larger part of their waking hours emotionally detaching from a workplace that their bosses and managers want them to wholeheartedly serve.

Why does detachment germinate time and again? With the many layers of management plus management initiatives most companies put into place, why are the "managed" workers so uncommitted to the company's success? What are the challenges that lurk inside a bureaucratic organizational structure? Why doesn't bureaucratic management seem to work, and what, precisely, *is* "management," anyway?

The Truth About Management

Management, quite simply, is how things have always gotten done. It's how the Egyptians built the pyramids, how the Chinese built the Great Wall of China, and how we set up Project Apollo and put a man on the moon. Everything that is accomplished in the workplace or in our daily lives is accomplished through management of some sort. Yet, there are various types of management. The pyramids and the Great Wall of China, for instance, were built by slavery, the ultimate in command-and-control management. All other examples of formalized (workplace) management in our Western culture are based on association with organizations, bosses, managers, and supervisors.

If we visualize a linear continuum of management, we could say that command-and-control management (the form of management inherited from the military, and typical of organizations with bureaucratic hierarchies) lies in the middle. That puts slavery at the beginning, while pure self-management (the way people manage their own lives on a daily basis) falls at the end.

Most shades of formalized management represent some form of command-and-control that relies on certain levels of force or coercion to prod people into doing the jobs they found themselves with. No surprise, then, that the legal language of master and servant still seems glued to the center of the continuum. Phrases such as "slaving away" at the office or being paid "slave wages" are as commonplace as ever.

"Employee," defined by Dictionary.com as "a person working for another person or a business firm for pay" is still the most frequently used word for a peer in the workplace, although it is extraordinarily outdated. (Certainly, no millennial will tell you her life's goal is to labor for someone else when what she seeks is purpose and meaning to her work.) Managers still refer to "direct reports" and "human resources" as though they were not human beings at all, and "headcount" and "manhours" as though no bodies are attached to the work that gets magically done. Yet, in the world of management, dehumanizing language is not happenstance; it is taught and perpetuated, designed to keep managers from relating to their subordinates as human beings brimming with creativity, ideas, and enthusiasm for contribution. After all, it's messier to control people than objects, and where management is concerned, a certain level of detachment makes things neater.

On the right side of the continuum (where in their daily lives people are somehow able to accomplish what they need to), humans buy homes and cars, raise children, and manage home inventory and purchasing. They move across the country or the world. They navigate the ins and outs of finance, insurance, health care, and more.

Management in daily life is fluid. It involves a good deal of networking and pact-making, and it ignites the creative spark in many of us. More than that, it requires us to constantly change direction as needed, retool as required, and re-affiliate with new partners and contacts for new tasks. In our daily lives, most of us are not only self-managers, we are also shape-shifters, somehow becoming whatever we need to be at any given moment.

Still, in the world of daily life, management is not predictable or static. Undoubtedly, daily life is not a precise and controlled place. And yet, things get done, often in highly innovative ways and with a good amount of commitment and even joy. People find others to assist them and agree to help one another; they make sure the kids get picked up from school and fed at dinnertime. They even corral the whole family for an intricately plotted holiday road trip. Management in daily life is fluid. It involves a good deal of networking and pact-making, and it ignites the creative spark in many of us. More than that, it requires us to constantly change direction as needed, retool as required, and re-affiliate with new partners and contacts for new tasks. In our daily lives, most of us are not only self-managers, we are also shape-shifters, somehow becoming whatever we need to be at any given moment: nurse, coach, furniture maker, chef, car mechanic, deck builder, fashion consultant, you-name-it. It's not a controlled state of existence, in the least. And yet, somehow, it works, and *things get done*.

Getting things done is management.

41 TELL-TALE SIGNS OF BUREAUCRATIC BREAKDOWN

Check the list or (if brave) ask a random sampling of workers to give you anonymous feedback. How many items below are realities in your workplace?

1. People quit frequently

2. Long hours are a way of life

3. People are unlikely to take initiative or innovate

4. Failure is unacceptable

5. Putting out fires has become routine

6. Workplace toxicity is often evident in online discussion and even in-house

7. People are not likely to renew and refresh their knowledge, skills, and abilities

8. People "protect their own" and do not proactively seek and share information

9. Mentoring is not actively encouraged or programmed

10. People are too often not up-to-date in their area(s) of specialization

11. Creativity is not encouraged; "Just do your Job!" is the mantra

12. People here are expected to do things "the way they've always been done"

13. The organization does not provide resources to pursue innovation

14. People (unwittingly or purposely) undertake actions that adversely affect others

15. People do not easily or consistently communicate about work issues

16. People do not voluntarily help one another

17. People do not hold each other accountable without blaming·

18. People routinely become defensive or retaliate when being held accountable

19. People often complain that expectations are not clear and defined

20. Leadership does not rotate to whoever possesses the most expertise pertaining to a task

21. Work groups often have leaders not best equipped for the group's goals

22. People do not respond well to changes in direction

23. People cannot comfortably challenge processes, relationships, or strategies that may be outmoded

24. People frequently do not rise to complex challenges

25. Negotiating changes in work terms and conditions is frowned upon

26. Resources needed for tasks are limited and cannot be augmented easily

27. Decision authority often seems intractable, inappropriate, opaque, or unreasonable

28. People feel they have little control over their own work

29. People feel they have little to no input into choosing with whom they will work

30. Relationships are often characterized by people seeking to get ahead or curry favor

31. Most people do not feel their viewpoints are welcome

32. Short-term expediency is often favored over a long-term perspective

33. People are too busy to take the time and effort to earn the respect of others

34. People are not necessarily interested in setting good examples for others

35. People often do not know where they stand regarding their performance, unless it is review time

36. People do not generally know what measures and metrics pertain to their mission

37. People must work through departmental hierarchies to get things done

38. People are not ordinarily aware of other colleagues' activities that may overlap or impact them

39. New hires do not get up-to-speed quickly or easily, and must sink or swim on their own

40. The organization does not easily capture and share relevant process knowledge

41. People fear disciplinary action for their mistakes; coverups are commonplace

CHAPTER 2

BUREAUCRACY: 15 UNAVOIDABLE CHALLENGES

[Bureaucracy is] the most rational known means of carrying out imperative control over human beings.

—MAX WEBER, NINETEENTH- AND TWENTIETH-
CENTURY GERMAN SOCIOLOGIST, PHILOSOPHER,
JURIST, AND POLITICAL ECONOMIST

COMPANIES TODAY, AS YESTERDAY, must produce products and provide services that satisfy (hopefully, delight) customers, at a profit. Clearly the economics of being successful in the world have not changed, regardless of organizational system. Businesses must be able to address all stakeholders' needs, no matter what their organizational model.

Yet, in a bureaucratic organization, challenges are everywhere. For many a CEO, life often feels more like navigating a jungle river with crocodiles gliding just beneath the surface. Tribulations that have persisted for eons remain, while new, twenty-first-century challenges come on like gangbusters. And so, the crocodiles proliferate.

Challenge No. 1—Production and Sales

Production, sales, services, and distribution needs do not change, no matter which mode of organizational structure your company has adopted. It's still about human beings performing their work to deliver the products and services to the customer in a timely manner that is competitive or, in the best cases, superior to the competition and offering greater value. The key here is *perception of risk*, for bureaucratic managers faced with the prospect of self-management often say, "This is scary! If I am not pushing my sales, distribution, and production staff to meet their quotas and minimum quality levels, how will that impact my metrics?"

Morning Star's Chris Rufer could answer that question, since his original aim was to offer the marketplace better value and service than did the existing tomato processors, and within a few years after the first plant opened, Morning Star did indeed command its industry space. Eclipsing the competition had a lot to do with high levels of engagement among the self-managed colleagues at Morning Star, which showed up in high retention rates and low turnover. Instead of the usual 67 percent of workers disliking their jobs or, at best, just going through the motions, Morning Star colleagues were usually striving to collaborate and innovate to find better and better ways to meet their customers' expectations—and in the process, make their own workdays interesting, rewarding, and even exciting as they also created new career pathways for themselves. Metrics trended upward as high levels of engagement translated directly into higher production throughput and improved customer service.

In bureaucratic organizations that rely on layers of management to perpetually prod and motivate ("How can we get people to do their jobs?"), challenges are everywhere as bosses are consumed by their people management issues and the resulting whack-a-mole impact on production, sales, services, and distribution. Even in the area of sales, where salespeople are generally more self-managed than anywhere else in the organization and interact directly with the customer, bureaucratic agendas and policies can wreak havoc. One only needs to think back to recent headlines of the 2016 Wells Fargo credit card scandal in which employees were motivated by sales incentives to create more than 3 million fraudulent customer accounts that also provided untold millions in cushy fees for the company. The damage to Wells Fargo's reputation is inestimable; its long-term competitive position in the marketplace is yet to be determined.

Challenge No. 2–Human Resources

It is impossible to approach this discussion without first asking the question, "Who is best qualified to find, retain, hire, assess, and, if need be, fire a particular worker?"

In a bureaucratic hierarchy historically constructed upon personnel policies and practices borrowed from government and the legal profession (and, if you think about

"Who is best qualified to find, retain, hire, assess, and, if need be, fire a particular worker?"

it, largely designed to protect business owners and managers from disgruntled or disruptive employees), the instinctive answer would be, "human resources, of course!" Yet, in the broad scope of life, it is those who will work side-by-side and/or collaborate with any given individual who are best qualified to understand the very specific needs of a job, its pitfalls, the type of personality best suited to the work, and more. Those working in tandem with others are also best qualified to know precisely how capable their hire is; after all, no eyes are closer to the tasks at hand. And if the newly hired individual is not working out or is having problems on the job, it is that new worker's colleague or colleagues who will notice the problems long before they become an unwelcome surprise that triggers a chain reaction throughout the enterprise.

On the other hand, a bureaucratic enterprise has plenty of policies and programs, added year after year, all designed to move employees through universal processes, whether they be hiring, firing, sexual harassment training, or whatnot. The problem with universal processes, however, is that they are one-size-fits-all, which, by defini-tion, reduces all company employees to a single common denomina-tor—usually the lowest. Such legalistic processes also keep people at arm's length, which means that management is often the last to know when something has gone awry with a particular employee. In bureaucratic organizations, the greatest challenge to human resources professionals is that, while they are congratulating themselves on moving their many employees through their authorized programs and processes, they have done little or nothing to address the 67 percent disengagement issue that lies at the heart of the company's struggle to succeed in its market space. Nor do those HR processes help to recoup hard-dollar production losses directly connected to employee disengagement.

I am frequently asked: Do self-managed companies reject their responsibility to legally protect their organizations when they hire and fire? My answer is: not at all, and they do not disregard the need for sexual harassment training and the like. Self-managed organizations simply strive to do these things in the most efficient manner possible, with the least impact on the mission of the business.

Challenge No. 3–Competitive Edge

Over decades, bureaucratic organizations have come to see the concept of competitive edge as a striving toward measurable goals, with growth at the forefront of those goals. Possibly, this striving toward measurable goals is just another vestigial appendage left over from military command-and-control. Yet interestingly, the word "compete" does not have its roots in the military. It comes from *competère*, Latin for "learning together, seeking together."

In self-management, competitive edge comes from individuals learning from other individuals and seeking solutions together. Business units collaborate with and learn from other business units, factories learn from other factories, and whole companies learn from external organizations. As Peter Senge describes in *The Fifth Discipline: The Art & Practice of the Learning Organization,*[7] the continuously learning organization

> *In self-management, competitive edge comes from individuals learning from other individuals and seeking solutions together.*

is at the heart of self-management, with competitive edge arising naturally from ongoing enlightenment and, thus, from continual improvement.

In the bureaucratic business world, however, companies set measurable growth goals to gain an edge in their marketplace. "Our goal is to grow revenues by 10 percent this year," or "We're going to grow sales by 15 percent over a year," are statements that set the bar for the

---

7   Peter Senge, *The Fifth Discipline: The Art & Practice of the Learning Organization* (New York: Doubleday, 1990).

organization as a whole and announce to global markets and share-holders that the company is in growth mode and, thus, is bankable. The problem is, when you set such goals, you also encourage shortcuts and taking any route possible to achieve those ends, which places integrity and the quest for excellence at the bottom of the company priority list. Anyone who followed the story of Enron, a monumental casualty of its own hyper-aggressive and unrealistic growth targets (among other things), would recognize this problem.

Funny thing is, customers *love* product and service excellence, and they are fiercely loyal to companies they can trust and believe in, which is all about integrity. Of the two routes to competitive edge—setting goals to be achieved by any means possible or creating an environment where excellence and integrity can thrive—the latter wins the edge, hands down. The alarming number of meltdowns exposed every decade in corporate bureaucracies determined to gain competitive edge through growth by any means bears this out.

Challenge No. 4–Strategic Retooling

Two questions:

1. How many five-year strategic plans have you worked on in your lifetime?

2. How many strategic opportunities has your company missed while you were involved in strategic planning?

You may think those two questions are not directly related, but they assuredly are. Strategy, as it turns out, is not about five-year plans. It is, however, all about *contingency* planning as you are watching the tides and currents of the marketplace and the world at large, and intimately sensing the winds of change. Strategy necessitates moving quickly and decisively as opportunities and risks arise.

Strategic retooling has everything to do with being nimble, quick on the draw, agile, flexible, and fast.

But bureaucratic organizations get too comfortable with their niches and processes and, at some point, lose any ability to strategically retool quickly and efficiently so they can promptly seize an opportunity or nimbly address a risk or threat. One must only look at the once-great market leader Kodak (The Eastman Kodak Company) to know that this is so. While the digital photography market was germinating, Kodak, which owned the patent rights to digital photography, could not mobilize its giant, slow-moving, and moribund bureaucracy to act. With its endless layers of management, processes, permission steps, and information channels, the company remained mired in the vanishing realm of film photography and allowed an entirely new industry to slip through its fingers—all while it held the key to that golden door.

Self-managed enterprises, on the other hand, are networked, action-oriented organizations that rely on natural and organic processes and, thus, can move and pivot with greater ease, as we'll discuss in the following chapter.

Challenge No. 5–Power

We can't acknowledge the mammoth hard- and soft-dollar costs of employee disengagement in conventional workplaces without admitting that the wielding of power plays a huge role. Just recently, at a job fair held by a new West Coast convenience grocer, Fresh Fill, twenty-something staffers put it to me plainly:

"We want to be self-managed because we're tired of working in places where people are hovering over us and micromanaging everything we do."

There's simply no underestimating the damage that the spirit-breaking control emanating from power can cause. Not to mention the sheer waste of human talent, skill, and creativity that result when a manager, supervisor, or colleague is more interested in exercising control (and coercion) than in getting out of the way and letting people do what they already know how to do everywhere else: plan, coordinate, select, budget, and organize.

There's simply no under-estimating the damage that the spirit-breaking control emanating from power can cause.

Power is addictive in the workplace. Evidently, we get a little jolt of feel-good dopamine every time we throw our weight around, says Ian Robertson in *The Winner Effect: How Power Affects Your Brain)*.[8] It also leaves a trail of business disadvantages. One significant obstacle to business growth and success is that while managers run roughshod over their subordinates, all sorts of valuable input and information is squelched. What's more, as power mongers in the workplace become more and more invested in their own egos, all sorts of other bad things start to happen, points out Dacher Keltner in *The Power Paradox: How We Gain and Lose Influence.*[9] One only has to scan the headlines as the daily parade of exposed and deposed power abusers in business, politics, and Hollywood marches before us. In the workplace, the psychological toll on company employees has connect-the-dot ramifications everywhere, including in most of the challenge areas I list in this chapter.

---

8   Ian Robertson, *The Winner Effect: How Power Affects Your Brain* (Great Britain: Bloomsbury, 2012).
9   Dacher Keltner, *The Power Paradox: How We Gain and Lose Influence* (New York: Penguin Books, 2016).

Power costs a lot of *money*, too. In fact, the price of the permission steps to decisions—the cost of moving information up and down the chain of command through management—is high (again, approximately half a *trillion* dollars annually, according to Gallup).[10] It is so high that American management expert Gary Hamel (author/coauthor of landmark business-strategy books, including *What Matters Now* and *Competing for the Future*)[11] has thrown down the gauntlet to American businesses. In a recent article, Hamel and co-author Michele Zanini challenged them to wring out the wasteful bureaucracy and dysfunctional bosses stifling workers and, by doing so, gain $3 trillion in additional output.[12] In the meantime, chains of command forged in pursuit of the mirage of control are shackling business performance everywhere.

Highly bureaucratic workplaces such as those within the investment banking industry may have scoffed at the accusations of power-based culture in the past, but they can't any longer. They simply cannot ignore the cost of control as millennials, and now Gen Z-ers, shun signing on or else flee not long after training (and the company's investment in them) is complete, as reported by numerous articles in *The Wall Street Journal* and elsewhere. According to Hamel, "The fault isn't with any particular leader, but with the top-heavy, bureaucracy-infused management structures that predominate in most organizations."[13] In fact, says Hamel, most CEOs do not realize that,

---

10   "State of the American Workplace," Gallup, 2017, https://www.gallup.com/workplace/238085/state-american-workplace-report-2017.aspx?g_source=link_NEWSV9&g_medium=TOPIC&g_campaign=item_&g_content=State%2520of%2520the%2520American%2520Workplace.

11   Gary Hamel, *What Matters Now* and *Competing for the Future* (Boston: Harvard Business School Press, 1994).

12   Gary Hamel and Michele Zanini, "Excess Management Is Costing the U.S. $3 Trillion Per Year," Harvard Business Review, September 5, 2016, https://hbr.org/2016/09/excess-management-is-costing-the-us-3-trillion-per-year.

13   Gary Hamel, "Bureaucracy's $3 Trillion Price Tag," Management Innovation eXchange, November 21, 2016, https://www.managementexchange.com/blog/bureaucracy%E2%80%99s-3-trillion-price-tag.

with their layers of unnecessary managers, they are in effect paying what amounts to a hefty "management tax," year in and year out. It's a cost of doing business they don't even need to incur.

Challenge No. 6–Management Tax: Hard-Dollar Cost of Bureaucracy

For those who find the discussion about the cost of bureaucracy too esoteric, Hamel's management tax is a right-between-the-eyes way to understand that fostering a bureaucratic workplace is all about dedicating huge sums of money to something *other* than core mission, competitive edge, and the timely and value-based delivery of the products and services. In truth, it's about sacrificing profit for something else entirely. I describe this tax to seminar and conference groups all over world and watch eyes pop open as I break it down for them as follows:

> Take a theoretical startup of ten people (the workers) making $30,000 each. Assume a management span of control of one to ten (real-world estimates of the average span of control vary, but let's keep it simple). Since managers invariably make more money than the people they manage, their boss or manager is probably making about $90,000 a year. If you amplify the existing management skills of those ten people, and give each of them a $5,000 raise, then you don't need the manager at all, and you've saved $40,000 annually. Scale that by a factor of ten and (with a span of control of one to ten), you have one hundred workers and ten managers, but you also need a manager for the ten managers. That person is making, probably, $200,000 a year. If you amplify the

management skills of the hundred workers, giving them each a $5,000 raise, then you don't need the ten managers and you don't need the manager of the ten managers, and you've just saved yourself $600,000 annually. Over a ten-year period, that's a net present value in the range of $3.5 million dollars—pretty compelling economics. And yet, bureaucratic organizations not only cling to their layers-upon-layers of management but, during recessions, they lay off *workers* and often hang on to their *managers!* Of course, this calculation often generates great fear and angst among managers (particularly middle managers), which we'll address later in the book.

DOING MANAGEMENT TAX MATH

100 people at $30,000 annual salary apiece	$3,000,000
10 managers of 100 people at $90,000 annual salary apiece	$900,000
1 manager of 10 managers at $200,000	$200,000
ANNUAL TOTAL	**$4,100,000**
100 people self-managing at $35,000 annual salary apiece	-$3,500,000
ANNUAL MANAGEMENT TAX SAVINGS	**$600,000**
MANAGEMENT TAX SAVINGS OVER TEN YEARS (NET PRESENT VALUE, DISCOUNT RATE OF 10%)	**$3,687,000**

Challenge No. 7–Innovation and Improvement

While companies like W.L. Gore nimbly and speedily innovate and improve, for organizations with entrenched bureaucratic management structures, improvement is sluggish, and innovation is often unknowingly (or, in the worst cases, deliberately) squelched by managers. Again, Kodak is the poster child here.

But as millennials and, next, Gen Z-ers populate the employment market, the tolerance for organizational listlessness and apathy evaporates. Toiling over trivial work for months or years to prove one's mettle merely to earn the opportunity to work on a major project or big deal doesn't cut it for these young people. They have little fear of starting up their own enterprises in the family garage, or else backpacking across Mongolia while they mull over their next steps and gain a worldly perspective in the process. The impact of these generational reactions has been earthshaking, most notably to long-entrenched sectors, such as investment banking, now completely disrupted by the millennials who either won't come onboard or won't stick once they're there. That sound you hear coming from Wall Street is the sound of scrambling: venerable firms are urgently rethinking their employees' involvement in the processes of institutional improvement and innovation, long held as rewards for only the most "proven."

Challenge No. 8–Attracting and Retaining Talent

Simply put, millennials (and the Gen Z-ers trotting along behind them) will not sign on or stay if they are not engaged in meaningful, purposeful work in the first weeks and months of their hiring. Companies of all kinds have come to realize that this means a thorough reassessment and overhaul of recruiting, hiring, onboarding, and training processes, if they wish to survive. As difficult as attracting talent has become, the even more painful issue is retention—not just because losing talent eighteen or so months into the process is so disruptive, but because it represents a huge waste of training dollars as millennials head to competitors or start up their own businesses with their newly acquired skills.

Challenge No. 9–Corporate Vulnerability

When I speak to bureaucratically organized companies about the soft underbelly they expose to their competitors, I always find it hard to mince words. I tell them straight out that their companies are vulnerable because they're sluggish, unwieldly, too heavy (and top-heavy, thus unbalanced), brittle, and ego-driven. There's nothing light, lean, nimble, adaptable, and open about them. Right now, Sears is literally vanishing before our eyes. The retailing pioneer, with a century-and-a-quarter of experience behind it, has been eaten alive by its online competitors.

Challenge No. 10–Workplace Toxicity

A persistent threat to organizations with conventional hierarchical models is that of massive workplace toxicity. Up until the advent of the internet and social media, the problem of disengaged, dissatisfied, and disgruntled workers existed (and always had), but did not necessarily pose an urgent or unmanageable threat. Certainly, a negative "word on the street" has always been undesirable. But to higher-ups, toxicity could be contained if it couldn't be ignored altogether.

These days, Glassdoor, The Great Place to Work Institute, The Job Crowd, and Vault (among other websites) provide transparent insider reviews and chatter about the realities of employee life at any given company. Companies invest surprisingly hefty sums in management consultants and reputation repair each year to try to counter the devastating impact on employee recruitment and productivity, not to mention consumer perception—all serious and possibly existential issues that directly impact the bottom line.

According to the reputation industry website, ReputationManagement.com, employers don't always realize that "losing out on top talent doesn't just hurt today: missing those great employees can be damaging for *decades* as you fail to capitalize on the great work they can offer." Seventy-six percent of job applicants, the site reports, are unlikely to accept a job offer from a company that has a bad reputation, even if the applicants are unemployed. (And the candidates who do accept ordinarily demand compensation higher than offered.) The more experienced the job candidate, the less likely to accept a position from a company with a dubious reputation. What's more, 93 percent of employees who *are* onboard would leave in a heartbeat for a firm with a good reputation, notes the site. LinkedIn surveys have shown he cost per hire is over two times lower for companies with strong employer brands, and that companies with stronger employer brands have 28 percent lower turnover rates than companies with weaker employer brands.[14] Those figures largely represent a survey of companies with conventional organizational hierarchies; we can only imagine what the expenditure would be in organizations where workers are not managed at all but manage themselves. What, for instance, would expenditures be like in companies where employees

---

14   Eda Gultekin, "What's the Value of Your Employment Brand?," LinkedIn, December 1, 2011, https://business.linkedin.com/talent-solutions/blog/2011/12/whats-the-value-of-your-employment-brand.

see their work as purposeful and inspiring, their career path as limitless as their company's potential for growth and success?

Then, too, there is the inextricable link between employee satisfaction and *customer* loyalty. Not every customer is privy to internal company reviews on Glassdoor, but *every* customer knows how well she has been served by the individual representing a given company. After all, to the consumer, that individual *is* the company. Toxic employees transmit their personal dissatisfaction with their company in endless ways, and customers are equipped with the antennae to detect that discontent even during the most meticulously scripted interaction. The connection between the absence/presence of workplace toxicity and consumer perception can be expressed by the equation: employee satisfaction=consumer loyalty=revenue. There are just no two ways about it.

Challenge No. 11–The Org Chart

Conventional organizations spend a great deal of time, money, and effort creating incredibly elaborate, complex, complicated, top-down organization charts in an attempt to tamp down all possible risk and uncertainty through the imposition of fail-safe command-and-control. For a good example of this, you can go to www.theofficialboard. com/org-chart/gm-general-motors to view the official, live version of General Motor's detailed organizational chart. Yet, aside from its nifty online format and some fairly standard 2017 graphics, it isn't much of a departure from GM's 1921 organization chart that follows:

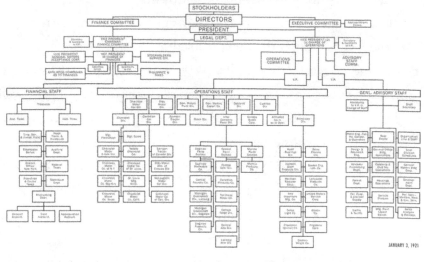

GM's org chart from 1921 isn't all that different from its current chart.

Back in 1921, GM executives struggled to manage and control their fledgling thirteen-year-old organization, and not much has changed almost one hundred years later, with one exception: subordinate org charts are doubtlessly abound in GM locations all over the world, as local GM bosses continue to employ complex measures to maintain control. Unfortunately, like most bureaucratic organizations imposing rigid organizational structures (and creating the charts to define them), the exercise only succeeds in snuffing out innovation, creativity, and flexibility, while creating a great deal of political and administrative maneuvering.

Organizational charting is the kind of activity that, along with the formation of a five-year strategic plan, can chew up plenty of resources and the good part of a work year.

Organizational charting burns up a tremendous amount of time and a good deal of work hours, and also involves a serious amount of people management as all levels of managers are moved around to where they would politically prefer to be or where their managers believe they should be. It's the kind of activity that, along with the formation of a five-year strategic plan, can chew up plenty of resources and the good part of a work year.

In the meantime, as management expert Gary Hamel has asked: *Why are you spending a ton of time and energy (not to mention money) doing "management stuff" when the effort is not creating value for your customers or adding to your bottom line?* The answer may have everything to do with fear, for companies that need everything etched in stone experience discomfort with the fluidity, constant movement, and shape-shifting emblematic of more nimble, robust organizations. Think of the difference between being on a fast-moving ship at sea versus sitting on a back porch: you'll feel more comfortable and less queasy sitting on the porch, but you won't get anywhere. The truth is, you'll have to experience some dynamism, movement, and, for a time, disorientation if you want to achieve anything.

Yet, learning to relinquish control so that your enterprise can move and change as needed requires a certain amount of brain rewiring for many people. According to emerging firms mentor and business philosopher Peter Koestenbaum (coauthor with Peter Block of the landmark book *Freedom and Accountability at Work: Applying Philosophic Insight to the Real World),*[15] this kind of rewiring is essential because in business, as in life, not only must we move, change, and grow, but we "must learn to *value* the pain of growing." All the time, energy, and money that companies spend creating organizational charts have never delivered them to their institutional goals. That's for a good reason, says Peter Block: "If there is no transformation

---

15   Peter Block, *Freedom and Accountability at Work: Applying Philosophic Insight to the Real World* (San Francisco: Jossey-Bass, 2001).

inside of us, all the structural change in the world will have no impact on our institutions."

Challenge No. 12–Incongruence with Twenty-First-Century Expectations

We've talked about how bureaucratic companies are finding themselves utterly out of step with millennials, and we have also touched on the impact of bureaucracy on competitive edge and corporate vulnerability or takeovers. All these things stem from bureaucratic rigidity and sluggishness, but also from an out-and-out incongruence with the twenty-first century. Companies mired in nineteenth-century organizational thinking and processes are still just plain out of step by about two hundred years.

When companies cling to the bureaucratic hierarchy models of the past two centuries, they also face the serious challenge of trying to meet twenty-first-century customer expectations with nineteenth-century service and process response. There are endless examples of companies that consistently disappoint and alienate their twenty-first-century customers. As consumers, we've all spent too much time on the phone with many of their customer service departments, or else trying to navigate their rudimentary websites. However, there is a perfect example of an enterprise that was specifically redesigned from a predecessor organization to fully meet twenty-first-century customer expectations. It is the world's largest home appliance manufacturer, dubbed one of the ten most innovative companies in the world: the China-based self-management icon, Haier.

Key to the Haier belief system is the tenet that "Users are always right; we need to improve ourselves." Haier's self-managed employees connect directly with end-users and, through the power of the internet (and via Haier's internet-enabled appliances), have immediate access to customer and market information. With this kind of advantage, the enterprise can serve customers quickly and well. Company workers demonstrate their value by making decisions as and when needed, by innovating and selling their concepts to colleagues and senior management, and by building teams to execute their ideas and share in the profits of successes. Most middle managers have been eliminated. Haier leadership reasons that because the workers no longer have bosses, they *must* listen to the users and be wholly accountable for outcomes. At Haier, the goal is to create zero distance between the enterprise and the customer. The objective is true twenty-first-century responsiveness to customer expectations, and it works because of self-management.

New York-based Meetup, launched in 2002, is another prime example of a company in lock-step with the expectations of its users, but it wasn't always so. Although Meetup was originally conceived as a niche-lifestyle venture possibly for fan clubs, Meetup's founder Scott Heiferman admits, "We were wrong about everything we thought people would want to use it for."

Today, after users found their own, more life-changing ways to use Meetup, the company has a simple and powerful idea at its core: to use the internet to get people *off* the internet, and back into personal interaction. Ironically, as the enterprise expanded, it fell into hierarchical patterns of management. So, leadership realized that Meetup's self-organizing *users* had it right: to succeed, the organization itself would need to be as autonomously managed as its users were. Then, with internal self-organization congruent with the company's business model, Meetup took off like a rocket. Meetup (purchased by WeWork in late 2017) now expects to hit one billion sign ups by 2020 because it is perfectly aligned with its self-organizing users and their twenty-first-century expectations.

Challenge No. 13–Blue-Collar vs. White-Collar Intelligence

For generations, blue-collar workers have been overseen by their white-collar managers. Frederick W. Taylor would have had no problem explaining that the disparity in levels of intelligence made this hierarchy not just necessary, but also that it was the nature of things. Taylor famously pointed out that an individual stupid enough to handle pig iron could certainly not possess the knowledge to grasp the science of handling pig iron. Yet, there is obvious fallacy in such a statement: Who, in fact, would be more likely to understand the characteristics of pig iron and the intricacies of its handling— someone who handles the material every day of his life, or someone with a textbook knowledge of the substance? Another fallacy lies in the assumption that because a worker is not college educated, he is *un*educated. This misconception is at the heart of the devaluation of trade education. It also underlies the theme of the book, *Shop Class as Soulcraft: An Inquiry into the Value of Work*,[16] by Matthew B. Crawford. In *Shop Class*, Crawford makes the case that America has lost something precious and essential by devaluing trade and encouraging everyone to get the "real" higher schooling of a college education.

In addition to the philosophical issues inherent in such a viewpoint, it turns out that we have created whole generations of middle managers not trained in any specific craft, while shortages of highly skilled tradesmen persist everywhere. This is because leaders

---

16   Matthew B. Crawford, *Shop Class as Soulcraft: An Inquiry into the Value of Work* (New York: Penguin Press, 2009).

of bureaucratic enterprises with rigid organizational hierarchies and top-down information flow (white-collar down to blue-collar) believe that those closest to their product and customer are *farthest* away from driving change and improvement. Their solution has been to build in more communication channels between management and the workers closest to product and customer: more layers of management.

In self-managed organizations, however, innovation is driven by anyone and everyone, and those closest to the product and customer often have the most valuable input. At Morning Star tomato-processing plants, for instance, the cognitive content of mechanics' and electricians' roles is often so high it is tantamount to that of a computer programmer in Silicon Valley, and the pay scale reflects it. Not surprisingly, innovation that can come from any working colleague at the company frequently is driven by blue-collar colleagues, no matter what their pay scale. They are free to make their case to colleagues of all types, including white-collar colleagues who would be involved in or impacted by the change.

White-collar managers herding blue-collar workers through their tasks may have worked in the nineteenth century, but, today, self-managed enterprises rely on *all* workers to keep them ahead of customer expectation and, importantly, the competition. A No-Limits Enterprise requires no-collar thinkers and doers.

Challenge No. 14–Fear, Anxiety, and Predictability

It is impossible to wonder at the persistence of bureaucratic organizational hierarchy in the workplace without looking at factors such as fear, anxiety, and predictability. Americans, especially, have a built-in bias for predictability. We all want foreseeable results. We want to meet our targets, goals, and key performance indicators (KPIs). It's all very linear. We want to feel in control, and we do *not* want surprises—especially bad surprises. (I have a friend whose anxiety is triggered by the very term, KPI.)

Certainly, this generates a good deal of anxiety in a conventional workplace, which can lead to an omnipresent sense of fear in general, seeping down through the many strata and landing on the individual employee. He wonders, *If this project doesn't work out, will I lose my stature in the company? My job? My house?* In companies with cultures that are anything but open and transparent, where communication is not free and is guarded, fear can surge in waves. Then, management's knee-jerk response is generally to institute more control, not plan for less. Anxiety and a need for predictability then spins out even *more* challenges: power-mongering, toxicity, serious retention issues, and the inability to attract talent to a fear-ridden, anxiety-provoking, over-controlled enterprise.

Challenge No. 15–The Future, and Human Beings in It

We have experienced an astounding amount of technological change and disruption in our lifetimes. Looking just over the horizon, we can see even more disruption to come in a very short span of time. The convergence of robotics and artificial intelligence (AI), plus block-chain, genetic engineering, nanotechnology, virtual reality, and all the rest, promise to be even more disruptive than was the internet. In their book *Infinite Possibility: Creating Customer Value on the Digital Frontier*,[17] authors Kim Korn and B. Joseph Pine II describe the new

---

17   Kim Korn and B. Joseph Pine II, *Infinite Possibility: Creating Customer Value on the Digital Frontier* (San Francisco: Berrett-Koehler Publishers, 2011).

world of technology and how it is creating infinite opportunities for innovation and customer value. We must start embracing the reality of that even newer world of technology, which is all about communication and information moving at the speed of light, enabling us to make decisions quickly. If, as business leaders, we create and foster organizations that don't allow that to happen, how do we hold any hope of keeping up with the future as it unfolds before us?

No, we can't know what the future will bring, but the one thing that we know for sure is that the eight primary commercial needs of human beings will not change, and every business in the world is organized to supply one or more of those needs: food, clothing, shelter, communication, transportation, personal security, entertainment, and health care. That's it. Whatever structures we, as human beings in societies, create to address those human needs, they will always require thought, creativity, and leadership, plus innovation and teamwork. Bureaucracy cannot get us there. It is incredibly costly in terms of resources and it impedes the fulfillment of those most basic human needs. The truth is, human beings are tired of bureaucracy, and it does not serve us well in the twenty-first century.

Above all else, bureaucracy in the workplace is wasteful of human life. If you are asking an individual who works within your enterprise to spend one-third of her life on nonvalue-added (in other words, worthless) bureaucratic tasks, then you are wasting one-third of that person's life. Multiply that life by

> *Above all else, bureaucracy in the workplace is wasteful of human life. If you are asking an individual who works within your enterprise to spend one-third of her life on nonvalue-added (in other words, worthless) bureaucratic tasks, then you are wasting one-third of that person's life.*

the tens, hundreds, or thousands of individuals who have pledged to serve your enterprise and who show up each day to do just that, and you are wasting an astounding number of years. Those are years of living, loving, sharing, and everything else that makes us human. At a certain point, we simply must examine the morality of wasting human life when there's not even a business benefit to the expenditure of those hours, days, weeks, and years. All in all, it is clear that bureaucracy does not facilitate the enterprise of the twenty-first century, but it only hinders it.

So, how can we make our enterprises stronger, more competitive, innovative, resilient, and intrepid as we move toward the future? How can we make workers happier and more fulfilled in the one-third of their lives that they spend with us? The answer lies, in large part, in the power of organizational self-management.

CHAPTER 3

THE POWER OF SELF-MANAGEMENT

Clouds form and then go away because atmospheric conditions, temperatures, and humidity cause molecules of water to either condense or vaporize. Organizations should be the same; structures need to appear and disappear based on the forces that are acting in the organization. When people are free to act, they're able to sense those forces and act in ways that fit best with reality.

—CHRIS RUFER, FOUNDER OF MORNING STAR[18]

TO BEST UNDERSTAND the power of self-management, we must first understand the principles and philosophies that drive it, and the differences between principles and philosophies.

The Power of Principles and Philosophies

As defined in most dictionaries, a principle is a *fundamental truth* or proposition that serves as the foundation for a system of belief

---

18   Frédéric Laloux, "Misperceptions of Self-Management," Morning Star, June 12, 2014, http://www.self-managementinstitute.org/misperceptions-of-self-management.

or behavior, or for a chain of reasoning. A philosophy, on the other hand, is a *theory or attitude held by a person or organization* that acts as a guiding principle for behavior. One can easily see how tightly linked principles and philosophies can and should be, especially as a business leader is pondering the best structure for an organization. A leader's *personal* life philosophy—say, that he believes his fellow humans should be happy in their work—can support a *fundamental* life principle, such as people must not be coerced (a fundamental principle of law in most cultures). Together, those fundamental principles and personal philosophies can inform the decision about what type of organization a company's leader would prefer to create.

As it turns out, the dual principles of noncoercion and keeping commitments to one another, however they may be stated, often form the underpinning of self-managed organizations. They are usually supported by the personal philosophies of company leaders; for instance, that people should be happy in their work.

> *The dual principles of noncoercion and keeping commitments to one another, however they may be stated, often form the underpinning of self-managed organizations.*

The first principle, that people should not coerce others, simply means that all interactions should be voluntary. This tenet, in fact, is the basis of law. Every law against murder, kidnapping, assault, blackmail, and the like, everywhere in the world, is predicated on the principle of noncoercion. It's a negative principle, representing something we should not do under normal circumstances. We recognize the power of this principle because, even though we accept the imperfection of people, we still can envision a world with no coercion, where armies and locks on doors would not be needed. We know the perfection of that vision is utopian, but we also know that the more closely aligned we are with the principle of noncoercion, the better off we are as human beings.

The second principle is that people should honor the commitments they make to others. It's a positive principle, representing something we should do. This principle is the foundation of civil law, especially contract law. Even as we seek remedy or restitution from those who fail to keep their commitments to us, we can still imagine a world where every individual does what he says he will do, and we know that world would be a wonderful place in which to live. We may never achieve a state where this principle is universally embraced, but we know that, as human beings, we are better off when businesses and organizations keep their promises to us.

Self-Management Is Everywhere

To say that self-management is "everywhere" does not mean everywhere in the business world; it means *everywhere*, for self-management naturally occurs across the flora of our planet and the entire animal kingdom of which mankind is part. In the world of plants, for instance, many ferns, shrubs, and grass species can "out-compete" trees and other tall-growing flora for nutrients and sunlight, because they grow close to the forest floor. Such vegetation is considered "self-managing" because it limits the presence of trees that would predominate, and it does so without the help of human or other intervention. Many ferns and shrubs even produce specific chemicals that keep other plants from rooting nearby.

One particularly fascinating example of self-management in nature is that of the Argentine ant (*Linepithema humile*), which scientists say has now become an ant mega-colony apparently colonizing much of the world and rivaling humans in its sheer scale of global domination. The Argentine ant mega-colony that originated in South America now spans much of the Mediterranean, California, and Western Japan; one super-colony alone reportedly covers 6,000 kilometers of Mediterranean coastline!

World-conquering Argentine ants appear to have a simple, two-pronged mission. First, to survive; second, to reproduce. Their mission, which they accomplish to perfection, is the essence of simplicity. As long as the ants focus on their mission, there are no apparent barriers to scale. To meet their dual mission, the colonies utilize self-managed division of labor and use chemical signals to communicate promising trails or threats to others. The self-managed actions are simple, efficient, and effective.[19]

Bees, too, rely on self-management in myriad ways. To distill powerful lessons for human organizations, David Zinger, founder of the Employee Engagement Network, launched a three-year study of honey bees. In his study, "Waggle: 39 Ways to Improve Human Organizations, Work, and Engagement,"[20] he notes the need for incessant communication (via a "waggle" dance) and collaboration among individual bees, which enables them to find food and stay connected with the organization. And Ken Thomson, in his book *Bioteams: High Performance Teams Based on Nature's Best Designs*,[21] describes alternatives to the conventional command-and-control model for high-performing organizations, derived from spontaneously organized bodies of critters that function and thrive all around us.

Yet, while self-management models exist across most species of life on our planet, it is self-management in our ordinary human

19   Matt Walker, "Ant mega-colony takes over the world," BBC, July 1, 2009, http://news.bbc.co.uk/earth/hi/earth_news/newsid_8127000/8127519.stm.

20   David Zinger, "Waggle: 39 Ways to Improve Human Organizations, Work, and Engagement," accessed January 17, 2019, http://www.davidzinger.com/wp-content/uploads/Waggle-by-David-Zinger.pdf.

21   Ken Thomson, *Bioteams: High Performance Teams Based on Nature's Best Designs* (Tampa: Meghan-Kiffer Press, 2008).

lives that should serve as our most powerful model. Left to our own devices, human beings naturally and organically organize, function, and make hundreds of decisions daily, all by themselves. People come together in civic groups, community organizations, nonprofit organizations, volunteer groups, churches, and meeting places, to get things done—all without any real command authority. They voluntarily collaborate and initiate a flow of commitments to one another and rely on each other to coordinate and manage as promised. Those few who self-select out or fail to meet their commitments do not deter a group that is focused on its mission.

Throughout command-and-control history, high-functioning self-management examples have abounded. Self-management has, for centuries, served tribes in which each member is expected to collaborate with others and keep the commitments made to peers and the group as a whole. In the latter half of the 1800s, for instance, the Native American Apache tribe of the Arizona Territory consistently outsmarted the US Cavalry by breaking up into small, decentralized bands of warriors and melting into the desert where they could not be detected, tracked, or eradicated by cavalry troops. (The command-and-control cavalry troops, on the other hand, were easy targets for self-managed Apache warriors, such as the notorious Geronimo.)

The Apaches and other decentralized groups like them are detailed in *The Starfish and the Spider: The Unstoppable Power of Leaderless Organizations* by Ori Brafman and Rod Beckstrom.[22] Brafman and Beckstrom use their powerful starfish/spider metaphor to make their point about organizational modeling for autonomy and adaptability: they explain that if you cut one leg off a spider, you have a dead leg and a seven-legged spider. If you cut off the spider's head,

---

22   Ori Brafman and Rod Beckstrom, *The Starfish and the Spider: The Unstoppable Power of Leaderless Organizations* (United Kingdom: Portfolio, 2006).

you have a dead spider. Yet, cut a leg from a starfish, and you have two starfish. Cut the head off the starfish and you have *five* starfish. Each part of a starfish, they point out, has the ability to regrow the rest. And so it goes with the adaptable and autonomous (self-managed) organization: with mission, commitment, and accountability, each leg has the capacity to regenerate any needed part of the organization.

In the world of quantum physics, too, which encompasses the principles of origins (matter and energy throughout not just our planet, but also the universe), molecules and atoms "collaborate" by attracting and disengaging as needed, creating the oscillations and vibrations that form the basis of life itself. Self-management, with the same as-needed engagement/disengagement design, is a natural, organic form of function for business organizations, because—just as it is throughout life on Earth—self-management is *everywhere*.

Self-Management: Win–Win in the Workplace

Clearly, no matter how the two core principles of successful self-management—noncoercion and keeping commitments to one another—are stated, they are also core principles of human life and law as we have known it throughout time. When he was designing his wholly self-managed organization, these were the two guiding principles that Morning Star founder, Chris Rufer, asked those who wanted to come on board to embrace:

> First, that Morning Star colleagues should not coerce each other to do anything: all their interactions should be voluntary. And second, that all Morning Star colleagues should honor the commitments they make to others.

As he was envisioning what his new Morning Star tomato-processing business would be like, Rufer's personal philosophy was (and still is) that to the degree individuals live by these two fundamental principles, they generally experience greater happiness and engagement. He believed that people perform better when they feel good about themselves, and that the enterprise would be the beneficiary of their happiness and involved participation in the workplace. In other words, the perfect win–win. He refused to be daunted by the fact that, up to that point, most businesses hadn't embraced these principles. Rufer believed the principles of noncoercion and keeping commitments to be foundational to people working together, and he considered them at the core of reputation, integrity, and trust—all essential not just for human beings, but key to the success of any company interested in keeping its customers.

Yet, what if business leaders choose to ignore such basic principles of human life as they design their companies' organizational structures? The funny thing about a fundamental principle of life is it exists and is always working *whether or not one chooses to heed it*. Like the irrefutable principle of gravity, a foundational life principle is always operational—whether tested, described, or ignored. What's more, just as with gravity, not aligning behavior with a life principle (and choosing to ignore it, instead) can have profound consequences. After all, you may choose to believe that you are not earthbound and can fly, but launching yourself off a precipice will quickly prove otherwise. Similarly, choosing to ignore a fundamental principle, such as not keeping the commitments that you make, can cause enormous damage. Notorious examples abound: Charles Ponzi's fraudulent promises of unrealistic arbitrage returns to his investors is only one.

While ignoring basic human principles carries serious repercussions and costs, *aligning* actions with principles conveys significant benefits—and therein lies the win–win for self-management. The same core principles of noncoercion and keeping commitments, that were proposed by Chris Rufer and adopted in 1990, govern Morning Star today. Approaching $1 billion in sales, the company has become the largest tomato processor in the world; its products are sold globally and consumed by virtually everyone in North America. Morning Star's colleagues somehow achieved these results from ground zero, by individually managing themselves without bosses, titles, or command authority.

How did they do it? They adhered to the principles of noncoercion and keeping commitments. And in their organizational planning, they focused on simplicity.

Simple, Elegant Workplace Solution

Visa founder Dee Hock said it best when he declared that simple, clear purpose and principles give rise to complex intelligent behavior, while complex rules and regulations give rise to simple, stupid behavior. Certainly, trying to navigate markets, develop strategies, satisfy customers, and meet the needs of all stakeholders is complicated enough without adding the additional complexity of elaborate management systems. Even within more conventional organizational hierarchies, great leaders have always known that finding the right people—and then getting out of their way to let them do what they do best—is key to business success.

Great leaders have always known that finding the right people—and then getting out of their way to let them do what they do best—is key to business success.

So, if all of that is true, why *wouldn't* you want simple, clear, fundamental rules and principles in place, wherein people can do what they do every day of their lives: manage themselves?

Consider this analogy: For decades, civil engineers in the US have been grappling with traffic flow issues—increasing, staggering, and timing traffic lights; escalating stop and yield signage; alternating street directions; and more. In the United Kingdom, however, engineers correlated the burgeoning use of such approaches not to improved traffic control, but to traffic interruption and backups. They then discovered that, with the institution of simple roundabouts, people would be perfectly capable of threading themselves through traffic intersections at even intervals without added layers of control devices. Stunningly successful, roundabouts proliferated across Great Britain and are now becoming more commonplace in the US. When you think about it, the sheer *time* wasted sitting at traffic lights during any one commute can really add up. Why should people give up hours of their lives weekly, when they can easily become accustomed to the simplicity of *not* being told what to do, and use their own judgment?

In the introduction to this book, I talked about Stephenie Gloden, an IT business unit leader at University of Phoenix, who decided that the simplicity of self-management principles would work well for her group. When her team's roadblocks were eliminated, her staffers discovered something else. Because self-management principles were so fundamental, natural, and straightforward, her colleagues were inadvertently incorporating them into every aspect of life *outside* of the workplace, too. Had the previous complexity of their business lives also been influencing the way the team members were relating to others in their personal lives? We can't know, but according to

Gloden, the simpler, more natural principles the team adopted at work made them happier human beings wherever they went.

The benefits of self-management are holistic and universal.

Moving Beyond Empowerment

When we consider the concept of self-management—wherein people interact, collaborate, and achieve under their own power without repressing, constraining, or coercing others—the question often crops up: Why not simply *empower* people to do what they do best? Why not extend *certain* modes of power to them, while retaining other types of control for the organization and its managers?

The answer lies in the true understanding of human nature, and in the acknowledgement that being a human has everything to do with choice and free will. Choice and free will can be repressed, but always at a cost. As a business leader, why pay that price—and force fellow human beings to pay an even greater price—when the ability of workers to exercise their free will and choice only *benefits* your company mission and goals?

Viktor Frankl, the Austrian neurologist, psychiatrist, philosopher, and author of the bestselling book, *Man's Search for Meaning*,[23] was also a holocaust survivor. His time in a German concentration camp taught him much about human survival, especially about the nature of human freedom. Frankl asserted that everyone has free will and, thus, everything is a choice. Even for a prisoner being led to the gas chamber in a concentration camp, he contended, free will exists: the prisoner can either go willingly to his death, or he can fight all the way to his final destination. Everything is a choice, said Frankl,

---

23   Viktor Frankl, *Man's Search for Meaning* (Great Britain: Rider, 2012).

even if people do not recognize the degree of freedom they have to make those choices.

Not recognizing that one has the freedom of will and choice does not mean that power does not exist. How many tyrants have made the mistake of assuming that because they have deprived people of the ability to *recognize* their own human capacity to choose, the free will may not surface once again as the people rise up and remove their despot from power?

For the Delancey Street Foundation, with six residential facilities around the country, free will is at the center of everything. The foundation was created in San Francisco in 1971 to help former drug users, convicts, and the destitute restore their lives through effective and accountable self-management. (Self-management became the structure of choice for the foundation administrators, too, not long after.) As part of the self-rehabilitation program, foundation guests are taught to act "as if" they are free-thinking people of integrity and trust, even if they have just spent months in jail for prostitution, murder, heroin possession, or the like. The irony is, these individuals *are* free-thinking people who have the will to do what they wish and make choices accordingly. Through life circumstances, repression, or self-denial, they have lost the ability to *recognize* that they have the freedom to make endless life choices—but that freedom is there, nonetheless. The Delancey Street Foundation does not empower its guests; it assists them in the brain rewiring they need to see that their own power as human beings is ever-present for their use.

Business philosopher Peter Koestenbaum applies the discussion of free will and choice to the enterprise as a whole and asks, *What does free will mean to the organization?* His conclusion: it means that everyone is responsible for motivating himself or herself, and it is not the job of company CEOs, leaders, and managers to motivate people.

CEOs, leaders, and managers may create the conditions and organizations in which people work, but people *self*-motivate, says Koestenbaum, and no one can successfully usurp that responsibility. The bonus win–win for organization leaders is that, once they recognize the motivational responsibility of the individual, they are no longer mired in empowering their people and shuffling them here or there to best uncover their skills or comfort zones. With workers finally responsible for unearthing their own power and negotiating (and renegotiating) their own positions within the organization, company leaders are at last freed up to deal with markets, strategies, and *their* responsibilities to the enterprise. The traditional management-model mind-set is, thus, turned upside down—or, possibly, right-side-up for the very first time.

For the enterprise, moving beyond empowerment involves opening the door to let a new kind of science sweep across the organization which, in turn, leads to changes in workplace language and culture. The shift in science involves a total departure from the linear, Newtonian thinking that inspired command-and-control in the bureaucratic workplace. That linear thinking is very up, down, north, south, and top-down driven. The new science that pervades networked, self-managed organizations is derived from a quantum world where, in the workplace, kinetic networks of people are in constant motion, shape-shifting as needed to anticipate and respond to need, nimbly and effectively. The Newtonian boxes in the conventional org chart, moved and troweled yearly to cement and recement control, are gone.

Dehumanized "direct reports" thus become the working partners that they are, and "human assets" make way for human beings—the difference between people and copier equipment not just acknowledged but embraced. As the business management authority Henry

Mintzberg says: "An enterprise is a community of human beings, not a collection of 'human resources.'"[24]

Finally, as organizations flatten, culture undoubtedly changes. But, with the advent of the millennial generation in the workplace, culture is already undergoing dramatic shifts, and so the question of ongoing culture change almost becomes one of the chicken and the egg: Does the "networked organization" drive culture for millennials, or do the millennials drive the culture change ahead, to further obliterate organizational structures? Or, is it both, simultaneously?

The fact of the matter is, millennials are not at all like their parents' boomer generation, whose members clocked their hours and paid their dues in the hope of climbing the corporate ladder without falling off. In their work, millennials don't seek to "get ahead" as boomers did; they seek purpose and the prospect of forging change in the world at large. They are driven by the ability to innovate, create, and collaborate, and are not at all interested in "slaving" for years to prove to their managers that they have worth. Millennials are like the atoms of quantum physics: they bounce around in a not-so-orderly fashion, attracted to the things they do best, pairing with other atoms to collaborate on specific projects, and then moving on to create whole chains of new interactions with vigorous results. With all the benefits to the

Millennials are like the atoms of quantum physics: they bounce around in a not-so-orderly fashion, attracted to the things they do best, pairing with other atoms to collaborate on specific projects, and then moving on to create whole chains of new interactions with vigorous results.

---

24   "Henry Mintzberg," Wikipedia, accessed January 17, 2019, https://en.wikipedia.org/wiki/Henry_Mintzberg.

enterprise derived from such powerful activity, the question is: Why would any enterprise leader or manager want to get in the way?

Power and the Social/Economic Win–Win

Not long ago, Robert Evans Wilson Jr., a student of motivation writing about the desire for power in Psychology Today, asserted: "Underlying the quest for power is fear, and the desire for power is to eliminate fear."[25] He went on to unequivocally state that, "political and social power is the ultimate form of control."

While I unquestioningly see the connection between power and control, until recently the connection to fear was not as clear to me. Then I encountered it, firsthand, in a consulting project that was extinguished by a mid-level manager working behind the scenes to harpoon her leader's exploration of organizational change. At the time, I was frustrated by the subterfuge that had been going on just under the radar, to quash any hope of the enterprise moving forward. I was disappointed for the enterprise leader who had the best of intentions but, in the end, knuckled under to pressure from a powerful (there's that word …) company executive.

Then I realized what was going on: the project had been jettisoned by an individual who feared the loss of her political power and, possibly, her management position within the organization. That fear and the desire to retain her political control eclipsed all else. In retrospect, I saw that she could not withstand the *discomfort* of her fear, engendered by the prospect of change. She sought control to assuage it and tamp down the change. In that she succeeded, at least for the time being. So, yes, fear and abuse of power go hand-in-hand, along with the desire to control others.

---

25   Robert Evans Wilson Jr., "Fear vs. Power," Psychology Today, March 11, 2013, www.psychologytoday.com/us/blog/the-main-ingredient/201303/fear-vs-power.

Still, power itself is not a negative thing. In a true self-managed organization, stakeholders and the workforce as a whole realize their full and individual power to engage in the mission of the enterprise, just as they do so in their own lives. They can choose to be disengaged and not interact, or they can choose to collaborate. But because every individual has a voice in a self-managed organization, that power can be checked. Even abuse of power—politicking, bullying etc.—may surface as long as people are human. Yet there is a greatly reduced tolerance for such behavior when all stakeholders own their own power, and everyone reaps the benefits of a business that moves to higher and higher planes. In the end, compelling economic and social benefits are a win-win for both enterprise competitive edge *and* human beings.

In *Haier Purpose: The Real Story of China's First Global Super-Company*,[26] authors Yong, Yazhou, Dearlove, and Crainer tell the story of a decrepit, state-run enterprise on the verge of bankruptcy, and how it became the world's largest appliance maker, absorbing American companies like GE Appliances. The story of Haier is very much like the story of Morning Star (which Haier CEO Zhang Ruimin studied as a model), except that Morning Star was a startup, launched to either sink or swim as a wholly self-managed organization. Haier faced the mammoth challenge of retooling an expiring dinosaur as a progressive, enlightened company moving toward self-management.

The leaders of both enterprises understood that power and control could play no role in the organizational designs of their companies, which would be focused on both economic and social benefits. Both companies would be driven by mission, values, prin-

---

26   Ha Yong, Hao Yazhou, Des Dearlove, and Stuart Crainer, *Haier Purpose: The Real Story of China's First Global Super-Company* (Great Britain: Infinite Ideas, 2017).

ciples, innovation, and initiative. In addition, both Haier's Ruimin and Morning Star's Rufer saw that top-down information chains were especially self-defeating to innovation and the ability to be agile. To enable such agility, they knew that information must be collected from the customers buying the product(s). It then followed that information must flow from those individuals in the organization who were closest to the customers. Both Rufer and Ruimin knew that these individuals would be the most important people in the world to customers. The old model of customer service employees waiting for direction from managers was dead.

Haier's Ruimin put it best when he described turning the information flow on its head to relentlessly drive innovation and improvement: "It is important to keep twirling the pyramid all the time, because it is more important employees listen to the market and not the boss."

Organizational Self-Management Is Global

There's no way to appreciate the impact of self-management in the global marketplace without looking at two prime examples: W.L. Gore and Semco.

Conceived in a Newark, Delaware, garage in 1958, and termed "pound for pound the most innovative company" in America by *Fast Company*,[27] W.L. Gore and Associates was the brainchild of entrepreneurial dynamo Bill Gore and his wife, Genevieve. The couple did not only develop the high-performance Gore-Tex concept that would later spawn Glide dental floss, Elixir guitar strings, and advanced industrial material, they also conceived the "lattice" organizational structure that made W.L. Gore one of the first basically flat

---

27   Alan Deutschman, "The Fabric of Creativity," *Fast Company*, December 1, 2004, www. fastcompany.com/51733/fabric-creativity.

companies in the world, and consistently one of *Fortune* magazine's "100 Best Companies to Work For."

Gore's global customers, which include Columbia Sportswear, The North Face, The US Department of Defense, NASA, and police agencies worldwide, are consistently loyal to a company they see as delivering amazing results, year in, year out. The company's flexibility and adaptability to the global marketplace can, in good part, be traced to its organizational structure. Gore's associates in research and development have the freedom to form flexible teams around specific research projects; they spontaneously band together to pursue particular innovations, then disband and form new teams based on new ideas to develop. Innovation can and does come from anywhere. Elixir guitar strings, for example, was a concept conceived during company "dabble time" by a musician who was also an associate in Gore's medical products division. Gore's four key principles, standing the test of sixty years, are Freedom, Fairness, Commitment, and what the company refers to as Waterline: Gore associates consult with knowledgeable coworkers before taking any "below the waterline" actions that might cause damage to the enterprise.

Unlike W.L. Gore, which constructed its business from the ground up on its visionary lattice organizational structure, the Brazilian company Semco Partners (originally Semco Group) moved to a people-centric organizational structure from rigid command-and-control. In 1980, after continually clashing with his son Ricardo, CEO and founder Antonio Semler handed over the reins of his troubled company to Ricardo, then aged twenty-one, and challenged him to save the business. At the time, the Brazilian equipment supplier reported annual sales of $4 million. Ricardo Semler immediately fired two-thirds of the company's managers, began to diversify the business, and, importantly, set about finding a better work–life balance for his company's workforce, while opening the company to innovation and growth. Twenty years later, through radical structural experimentation and daring diversification, he had grown the business to $212 million, with 40 percent annual growth and a less than 2 percent employee turnover rate.

Today, Semco Partners' reports annual global sales volumes of more than $1 billion annually across numerous industries. During a recent ten-year recession in Brazil, the company still grew 600 percent, profits were up 500 percent, and productivity soared by 700 percent, according to *Inc.*[28]

Semler has also applied his unorthodox, people-centric self-management ideas to schooling and other aspects of Brazilian life, as well. Behind this drive is his desire to help others think out of their boxes and better appreciate their lives, which he talks about in his books, *Maverick* and *The Seven-Day Weekend.*[29] Semler's focus on globalization, tech acceleration, change and, especially, economic dislocation (the disparity between the poor and the wealthy) has resulted in greater fairness in the workplace for his own people, who even determine their own salaries. Importantly, it has also spurred remarkable success for the enterprise itself. In a recent TED talk,[30] the irreverent Semler quipped, "People with a lot of money always talk about giving back, but maybe they took too much to begin with!" When asked about his uncanny ability to loosen the reins everywhere in the workplace and inspire trust that comes back to the enterprise in innovation, growth, and profit, he responded simply, "It takes a leap of faith about losing control."

---

28 Chuck Blakeman, "Companies Without Managers Do Better by Every Metric," *Inc.*, July 22, 2014, www.inc.com/chuck-blakeman/companies-without-managers-do-better-by-every-metric.html.

29 Ricardo Semler *Maverick* and *The Seven-Day Weekend* (New York: Grand Central Publishing, 1993).

30 Ricardo Selmer, "How to run a company with (almost) no rules," TED, October 2014, www.ted.com/talks/ricardo_semler_how_to_run_a_company_with_almost_no_rules.

W.L. Gore and Semco Partners are two outstanding examples of self-management in the global arena. Now driving global interest in self-management everywhere is what is known as VUCA: Volatility, Uncertainty, Complexity, and Ambiguity. As companies everywhere try to comprehend the best ways to adapt in a VUCA world, they are discovering, time and again, that self-managed organizations are proving to be the most nimble.

Welcome to a Future Designed for Self-Management: 11 Catalysts

For an overview of what the future of work looks like, test drive my **Interactive Periodic Table of the Future of Work**,[31] inspired by friend and science entrepreneur, Kennan Kellaris Salinero. Derived from it in part are eleven catalysts of future change that will help society transcend workplace bureaucracy. The catalysts for change include:

1. **Technology**—Arriving and imminent technologies prove to be more disruptive than the internet itself. The convergence of blockchain, artificial intelligence, virtual reality, genetic engineering, robotics, nanotechnology, and many others will astound. Today's disintermediators will themselves be disintermediated. Traditional employment structures will not be immune from change. People will demand that organizations be as flexible and creative as the people who work for them.

---

31   Doug Kirkpatrick, "Interactive Periodic Table of the Future of Work," LinkedIn, December 1, 2016, www.linkedin.com/pulse/interactive-periodic-table-future-work-doug-kirkpatrick-1/.

2. **Millennials and Gen Z-ers** resist bureaucratic working environments and flock to agile and flexible work environments of creativity and purpose.

3. **Communities, Member Associations, Networks, and Conferences** experience an explosion in sharing knowledge, practices, and experimentations, which drive innovation. Collaborative groups see experimentation "failures" as proof of their drive toward innovation, building credentials.

4. **Corporate World Co-Opts Agile Software Development Model**—Product and service development as a whole moves to software development's short-sprint, iterative model which relies on persistent user input.

5. **Social Technology Liberates Collective Intelligence**—Open Space, the World Café, and hundreds of other social technology practices augment conventional meetings and presentations and become foundational to self-management.

6. **Pracademia**—Academic insight moves to practical application; change emanates from visionary institutions such as Singularity University, The Center for Innovative Cultures in Salt Lake City, and The Center for Positive Organizations at the University of Michigan.

7. **Virtual Teams**—The worldwide phenomenon of collaboration among virtual, distributed teams continues to embrace synchronous and asynchronous self-management models.

8. **Journalists/Media/Blogs**—Journalists across business and mainstream media increasingly chronicle and forecast the rapidly changing VUCA world and spread the word: companies must pay attention and be agile! Numerous bloggers and podcasters serve as the frontline reporters on the future of work (see, for example, Medium.com.).

9. **Network Mapping**—Organizational charts go the way of the dinosaur as enterprise workforces self-organize and organizations track organically formed processes, innovators, and influencers to better understand human networks. (World Bank and United Nations use Net-Map, a flexible and open framework for understanding networks.)

10. **New Products and Services**—New technologies enable teamwork and collaboration, and streamline networking and cultural understanding through decision support, messaging, polling, surveys, metrics, etc., making time, place, and matter irrelevant. (For example, check out Waggl, Slack, Ryver, CultureAmp, and many others.)

11. **New Science**—The new, nonlinear workplace echoes the quantum world of cause-and-effect rippling and cascading waves, requiring real-time responsiveness. The Newtonian world of linear directives from bosses begins to disappear.[32]

---

32   Margaret Wheatley, *Leadership and the New Science* (Oakland, CA: Berrett-Koehler Publishers, 2006).

CHAPTER 4

BEFORE YOU PLAN: SELF-MANAGEMENT CONSIDERATIONS

Innovating the organization's structure itself is the last frontier of strategic and competitive advantage.

—**DOUG KIRKPATRICK**

NOW, LET'S SAY YOU ARE BEGINNING to see the constellation of strategic, competitive, and human benefits that can accrue to a self-managed enterprise. You are considering the concept of self-management as a viable alternative as you guide your company into the future or launch your new venture. But—wait. You have so many questions, and while some are entirely logical, others may have more visceral origins. After all, this is *change* we are talking about. Change can be exciting and teeming with promise, yet it can also breed fear within an organization if it is not managed properly.

Before any internal discussions can take place (and certainly before you make the case for self-management to stakeholders), it is vital to confront questions, apprehensions, and preconceived notions about self-management as an organizational philosophy, and in practice. To facilitate the discussion here—and discussions you will be involved in within your own organization—I have provided a comprehensive list of frequently asked questions (FAQs) and my responses to them. An experienced self-management advisor can help you with the many, many additional questions your stakeholders may pose about your particular enterprise (for example: Which of our colleagues will handle strategy? How, precisely, would our company handle compensation? What will the managers we keep onboard be doing? How long will our specific initiative take to roll out?). The answers will depend greatly upon the scope of your initiative, the size of your enterprise, and the extent of the change you hope to initiate with each phase of your implementation. If you are serious about the prospect of moving to self-management, all issues should be discussed with stakeholders up front, to prevent unnecessary anxiety about change that is being considered.

Moving to Self-Management: The Most Frequently Asked Questions

Q: Moving to a self-managed organizational structure sounds pretty much like inviting chaos to reign as people "manage" themselves. What if we adopt self-management, I lose control, and chaos or even anarchy results?

A: Whenever I hear these very valid concerns as I am meeting with company leadership, I suggest that if their engagement levels are typical of the American workplace, 67 percent of their workforce is already disengaged—basically, not inspired to produce. I ask: "With all that disengagement, do you have chaos right now?"

"Well, no," they usually respond.

So, even with a workforce that is not fully engaged, not producing as anticipated (and, thus, not controllable), chaos hasn't yet taken over. That's when I say, "Well, if you engage these individuals in self-management, every single one of them will have a purpose and clearly identified responsibilities. What's more, every person will know how to measure his or her own success, and will have the well-defined right to speak up, innovate, and negotiate his or her activity within the organization and among peers. Everyone will be directly accountable to everyone else, to a personal commercial mission, and to the mission of the enterprise. In other words, the organization will be operating under greater, more widespread control than it did under the single-command ladder of a traditional hierarchy. It could actually be a *safer* environment for the business, because with everyone accountable to everyone else, a much more robust system of checks and balances exists. Does that sound like a scenario of organizational discontent and chaos ripe for anarchy? Or—" I ask (sometimes casually tossing *Fortune's* "100 Best Companies to Work For" on the table), "does that sound like a wonderful place to work, where people would want to do their best?"

Having said all that, the chaos question is completely legitimate. No organizational change must be allowed to create chaos. A polarity must be managed between moving so slowly as to make real change imperceptible, and moving so quickly that real chaos ensues. Involving people in the creation and shaping of the change from the outset, to create a sense of stewardship, is a critical success factor.

Q: I'm in middle management. If the company moves to self-management, what will happen to me? Will I lose my job?

A: When a company moves to self-management (as opposed to a company launching from the ground up as a self-managed organization), this is a legitimate concern. My response to anyone in a management position is: "What is your expertise that is valued by the organization, and why would the organization *not* need that expertise, regardless of its organizational structure?" In other words, if you are a subject matter expert contributing value to the organization, why would the need for that subject matter disappear? On the other hand, if your job is solely to tell others what to do, then, yes—there might be less of a need for your services.

This, of course, throws a spotlight on just about everything that has gone wrong with bureaucracy in the workplace over the decades. People with perfectly good skills and expertise in all sorts of areas—areas in which they studied, trained, and apprenticed—were gradually moved into "people management." Not surprisingly, the number of well-intentioned workers who ended up managing other people (while still longing for the day that they could return to the occupations they originally envisioned for themselves) is legion. What's more, it turns out that managing people, versus applying subject matter expertise to a business domain, requires a completely different skill set. The "people managing" skill set essentially relies on a wholly different part of the brain. This may explain why so many people fail as managers. A young woman may start out as an architect in an engineering firm, for instance, and be recognized as a terrific engineer. Yet, before she knows it, she's expected to manage a team or a workgroup. She never quite rises to the management challenge and, in the meantime, she wonders why others are now doing the architectural work that she loved.

But there is a business solution for this conundrum, and it's all about *splitting off* the role of the manager; that is, redesigning roles so that people can focus on their subject matter expertise. Or, if their expertise lies in working with people, they can focus only on that. Companies, then, no longer expect large numbers of people to become managers *in addition to or instead of* their areas of expertise. (To find out more about this business model, go to peoplecentricorg. com, the People Centric Organizations Group.)

For the business leader reading this book, the two middle-manager questions, "What will happen to me? Will I lose my job?" are not only critical for the managers voicing their concerns, but are important to the success of the self-management initiative as a whole. If these completely understandable concerns are handled proactively and thoughtfully, then the initiative can stay on track with minimal disruption. Those in unnecessary people-management positions can then be assisted to find new or renewed purpose with as little upheaval as possible.

Q: What if our employees express fear about a self-management initiative?

A: Again, with change (even with *rumors* of change that may be in the offing) comes fear. That's just human nature, and it is important to realize that there is no way around it. People have always been fearful of the unknown, and action generated by such fear is rarely positive action. So, the key here is to get in front of that fear, and do it in a personal, not *im*personal, way. After all, to a company employee, uncertainty about his or her future is personal.

This means you will need to have conversations, and a lot of them, perhaps exhaustively—with teams, with groups, one-on-one, any way that you can. Importantly, the discussions will need to be *two-way* discussions, for the fears are going to crash through in the early stages of those conversations, and they must be addressed and not taken lightly. Even if fear is not being outwardly expressed, you should always assume fear exists nearly any time widespread change is taking place inside an organization. Warning: if you are not listening for fears, they may be doing greater damage to your self-management initiative than you know. That brings us to ...

Q: What if there is under-the-radar resistance to our self-management initiative? How can we know about it, and how can we prevent sabotage and toxic behaviors?

A: It can indeed be difficult to know about under-the-radar resistance, especially if you are assuming that everyone is on board from the outset. In Chapter 3: The Power of Self-Management, I recounted my own experience with a client company whose senior management had come to me to help them move toward self-management. It was late in the game when I discovered that a single middle management individual had been quietly working against the initiative while we were trying to advance it. The CEO was a more reticent individual who eventually knuckled under to pressure that manager generated regarding the loss of decision rights (power).

I drew many lessons from that experience, the most important of which was: the company leader or leaders must be *fully* bought in and engaged from the get-go and engaged on a consistent and active basis. There can be no doubt about the company leadership's wholehearted commitment to this change. With organizational change this pronounced, a company leader cannot passively stand back in the shadows of the change initiative and simply observe as things evolve. The company leader(s) must be hands-on, actively promoting and actively involved all the way. If he or she is not willing to be wholly committed to the self-management initiative, then it should be halted; otherwise, it will be a waste of time. And if out-and-out resistance (even less-overt passive-aggressive resistance) is detected within middle management, it must be addressed speedily.

So, leadership that is not 100 percent on board and enthusiastically involved is a red flag. Another red flag of less-than-enthusiastic leadership support: team members who are not interested in finding out everything they can about self-management—reading, researching, touring other facilities, etc. Remember, to grow a solid initiative of ever-widening circles, you'll need "bees" (those who are solidly behind the effort) to go out, do their "waggle" dance, recruit other bees, and so forth and so on.

Q: What about employee fallout? What about those individuals who simply are not comfortable with self-management, and decide to leave the company voluntarily?

A: Employee fallout on some level is to be expected. While I can point to the countless ways that self-management is good for every business and everybody, the reality is that some individuals may not appreciate full responsibility, accountability, and the worlds of possibility that go along with that kind of opportunity. I genuinely believe that even the most introverted individuals eventually blossom when they take advantage of their power—their right to be heard, to contribute, and to innovate. But I also acknowledge that people within a group or organization may feel ready for change at varying times and need to seek out a more familiar type of organizational structure until they adjust to new levels of freedom. For some people, being able to speak up when needed involves psychic demands that just aren't comfortable. Such individuals may see the rigid organizational structure of a conventional work environment as security—even as it deprives them of certain rights they exercise daily outside of their workplace. You'll need to work through the fallout, not be taken aback by it, and handle it as gracefully as possible. That may involve helping people find alternative work situations that better meet their needs.

Q: The process of bringing ever-widening circles of company members on board sounds challenging and lengthy. What, precisely, is involved?

A: It's rare that the idea of self-management is "sold" to a single individual who then decides on behalf of an entire enterprise to alter the organizational model. One person may bring the idea to the table but, generally speaking, a leadership team becomes interested or else a company leader convenes a leadership team to look at the prospect of self-management. The team members may do a lot of reading and research on the topic. If they are serious, they may bring in a consultant to walk them through the concept and the various models in existence, before a commitment is made and more extensive work ensues.

The amount of time and the number of meetings it may take before company leadership decides to move ahead with a self-management initiative varies widely. Some teams bounce the idea around for months, taking into account potential resistance (and resisters), before deciding to make a commitment. Other leadership teams quickly move to a realization that self-management is their future. Recently, I was called in to meet with the leadership team at an education startup. The CEO was extremely motivated, and the team had done a good bit of homework. When I arrived, I was told outright, "We want to work with you, so let's talk about what this organization is going to look like."

Usually, however, the idea of self-management germinates and then is fostered through ever-widening meetings that require persuasion, persistence, and commitment on the part of the leadership team, plus numerous discussions about how to deal with the employee resistance that may be encountered along the way. In fact, smart leaders *proactively* look for the resistance early on, so they can decide how they wish to handle each instance. You can't talk in circles forever about resistance, for it can seriously thwart any organizational change a leadership team has in mind.

Q: Will moving to a new organizational structure such as self-management be a labor-intensive process?

A: The process of designing a brand-new organizational structure for your enterprise does involve a distinct amount of labor up front. The continual, ever-widening discussions that we have already mentioned are the first part of that work. The drivers of the organizational change will be looking for "hybrids": those individuals within the organization who can help shift the culture because they understand the existing culture, yet also understand the vision of the new ethos.

In addition, the *language* of the enterprise needs to change subtly, but significantly. Earlier in this book, we looked at the word "employee," which literally means "a person who works for someone else, for pay." We talked about "direct reports" and "human assets"—age-old HR terms that refer to human *beings*, yet were purposely designed to reinforce command-and-control, not inspire creative, innovative humans to reach new heights. The self-managed enterprise must carefully consider its language and conceptual framework, including the inherently dehumanizing idea of "human resources." These efforts take time and require careful thought.

Then, carefully designed tools and resources are essential to smooth and clarify the process for

> *The self-managed enterprise must carefully consider its language and conceptual framework, including the inherently dehumanizing idea of "human resources."*

all, ensuring that self-management is successful. Core to the groundwork required is the concept of written, mutually ratified "peer agreements" or contracts between those who are collaborating toward goals for the enterprise. We will discuss and illustrate these agreements in detail in Part II: The Self-Management Roadmap. Basically, the idea of peer agreements hearkens back to the central principles of:

- **Noncoercion**. No one tells a company member what to do; peers *negotiate* and *renegotiate* their work agreements with one another, and then negotiate with other colleagues as they move on to new or additional collaborations.

- **Keeping commitments**. Company colleagues are wholly accountable to each other and the enterprise as a whole; what they promise to do, they do, or else mutually renegotiate as conditions change.

The peer agreement is a contract that carefully identifies an individual's purpose and the content of the work, in terms of what that person is responsible for (you can find an example of this kind of agreement in Chapter 10, Bringing Self-Management to Life: 12 Real-World Components). It identifies the scope of decision-making authority in a way that connects and fits with everyone else's decision-making authority. In addition, it details how that individual will be measuring his or her performance, because there won't be a boss dictating that anymore. Any one individual may have agreements with three other people or even twenty-five others, all detailed in his or her contract. And those individuals will have their own agreements, negotiated with others. Across the enterprise, the networks of contracts (actually, social negotiations) will shift and change as the challenges do. Moreover, colleagues within the company will be continually sensing and responding to change in the workplace, marketplace, and world—all of which informs change and growth within the networks of agreements.

When you think about it, this kind of social negotiation is precisely what most of us do in our daily lives with repair people, service providers, neighbors, and family members—except that we don't always get it in writing. The peer agreements in a self-managed work environment, however, make every individual's work explicit; that is why I always advise they be utilized. All members of the enterprise are completely clear about what they are doing, and why they are doing it. The tangible, explicit agreements not only eliminate confusion and misunderstanding, but they also paradoxically free their owners to experience a level of tacit, intuitive awareness, and understanding that often does not exist in conventional organizations.

The best news is that all of this up-front work ensures a *self-perpetuating* process. In other words, implement self-management well and your days of reorganizing, org-charting, finding workarounds for endless management issues, and adding more layers of management are finally over. Most importantly, as the enterprise community continually creates its own networks of collaboration, engages in rapid experimentation, sets its own goals, and builds its own pathways to achieve them, the enterprise itself becomes an ecosystem for boundless success. Transparency and clarity drive accountability. The organization truly becomes a No-Limits Enterprise.

Organizational self-management should be incredibly liberating for traditional managers. If two former subordinates have a conflict, one can simply hand them a conflict resolution process and wish them luck—It's *their* job to work it out.

Q: Moving to self-management seems like it would be counterintuitive for many company leaders who have enjoyed their command authority. Yet, I hear about more and more CEOs looking at self-management models. What is motivating them?

A: A multitude of issues are in the forefront of organizational change today, not the least of which are competitive edge for the enterprise, ongoing hiring and retention issues (notably where millennials and upcoming generations are concerned), widespread employee disengagement and malaise, productivity issues, and a desire to retool the organization to be more and more nimble as the twenty-first century moves forward. Some CEOs look at their company software teams, which are already developing proprietary products within the agile development model and constantly interacting with the workforce and others, to improve and innovate. They wonder why the entire enterprise cannot operate on a similar model and become more creative and responsive in the process.

Other, more immediate or personal issues are also drivers of organizational change, and they often motivate CEOs to move quickly. Recently, I was contacted by a company founder nearing retirement who told me that he wanted his company to remain healthy and profitable for decades to come. He viewed self-management as the best possible way to create a resilient organization that was not dependent on finding the perfect successor CEO—a search that had been challenging up to that point.

Companies interested in merging or being acquired have shown increasing interest in moving to self-management, as well. They understand that bureaucratic organizational models are now globally recognized as burdened with employee disengagement and associated issues that tamp down growth and endanger future competitiveness and even the very viability of businesses.

And, empirically speaking, humanity is a prime motivation, especially for today's enlightened leaders. As we move into a more-informed era of people seeking to better balance work with the rest of life, entrepreneurs launching companies, and those revamping their organizations are taking work-life balance very seriously. They are appreciating that those who are happy in their work, work best. They understand that human beings fulfilled in their work lives carry that gratification into their communities and the rest of their daily lives, making a better world for all. Not coincidentally, self-managed companies become environments where—through engagement and love of the work—greater value is created, and thus greater benefits are reaped by all: customers, workers, and company owners.

Q: Self-management sounds like something that Silicon Valley would be interested in. It sounds pretty "granola" to me—a socialist or communist notion that is ethical but ultimately unprofitable.

A: A self-managed enterprise can be one of the hardest-driving, hard-core business-focused, number-crunching, bottom line-oriented businesses you can imagine. One look at the organizational model of uncompromising self-management (the tomato processor, Morning Star) reveals all. This is a company that launched in a market niche with plenty of competition and yet quickly rose to eclipse its competitors and emerge as the foremost tomato processor in the world. Though it was launched in a very traditional industry, the company's owner—Chris Rufer—believed that, with the help of self-management, his company would surpass the competition in productivity, innovation, and customer service. And he was right. So was W.L. Gore's Bill Gore, and Haier's Zhang Ruimin. All three company leaders (and others like them) had the success of their businesses top of mind. The fact that they believed that the route to success could be traced through the mutual fulfillment of enterprise *and* workforce has everything to do with an understanding of human beings and their needs and aspirations, plus a deep belief in core principles. While workers remain largely human, that seems more like common sense than anything else.

Next Up: Your Self-Management Journey

Yes, planning radical organizational change can seem like an overwhelming proposition, but it doesn't have to be. In the following chapters, you'll go on to quickly acquire:

- **A sense of where your organization will fit** along the self-management continuum.

- **An armada of real-life self-management models** to review.

- **Strategic and tactical how-to and tools** you will need to implement and launch your initiative.

- **A rundown of self-management implications** (what you can expect to occur on your journey).

- **Solid guidance to help you make the case** for self-management to stakeholders across your organization.

- **Real-world best practices** from today's self-management leaders.

By carefully considering options, resources, tools, and implications—the challenge can be exhilarating and rewarding on countless levels. Your self-management inspiration and journey lie just ahead in Part II.

PART II

THE SELF-MANAGEMENT ROADMAP

*An employer is good only for providing
the sandbox in which to play.*

—EDGAR H. SCHIEN, FORMER MIT SLOAN SCHOOL
OF MANAGEMENT PROFESSOR AND AUTHORITY ON
ORGANIZATIONAL CULTURE AND DEVELOPMENT

CHAPTER 5

NEW WAYS OF WORKING

The work of business is making and keeping commitments.

—FERNANDO FLORES, CHILEAN ENGINEER, ENTREPRENEUR,
AND POLITICIAN WHOSE WORK WITH ACTION WORKFLOW AND
COMMITMENT MANAGEMENT THEORY HAS BEEN FOUNDATIONAL
TO ORGANIZATIONAL CHANGE IN THE WORKPLACE

BECAUSE SELF-MANAGEMENT in the business world is all about keeping commitments—to customers, to the company mission, and among all those who collaborate in the workplace—commitment-keeping is key to any type of self-governing enterprise, no matter where it falls along the continuum of work environments. Frankly, keeping commitments should be the aim of any organization if the business owners want the enterprise to remain viable and competitive. Even in a highly repressive work environment, most business owners want to keep their commitments to customers and the marketplace. It's just that conventional bureaucracies usually rely on command-and-control to *compel* their workers to keep those commitments for them. But that's coercion, and it doesn't work very well for any extended length of time.

From Slavery to Salvation

When we look at the continuum along which organizational structures lie, what we're essentially looking at is varying degrees of coercion versus varying degrees of freedom in the work environment. The most-extreme example of that continuum would show us the most repressive work environment on one end, and a work environment that represents the model of total self-management (freedom to produce, create, and innovate with no command-and control whatsoever) on the opposite end. It would probably look something like this:

TOTAL COMMAND AUTHORITY TO ZERO COMMAND AUTHORITY

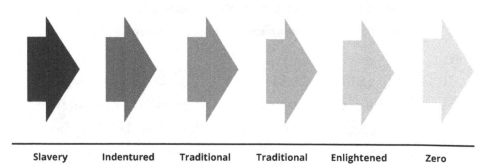

Slavery	Indentured Servitude	Traditional Employment: No Worker Protections	Traditional Employment: Worker Protections	Enlightened Employment Practices (Empowerment)	Zero Command Authority

In slavery, bosses rule and workers have no rights whatsoever, not even the right to command a wage for their labor. In a self-managed business such as the model of the wholly self-managed enterprise, Morning Star, there are no bosses and no managers of others. (The irony is that in a purely self-managed organization, there actually *are* bosses everywhere, for every company worker is accountable and answerable to every colleague across the enterprise.)

Therefore, when you are thinking about your own company's interest in self-management, you are doubtlessly going to be concerned about the issue of control: Who, ultimately, will control the organization? Will it be completely self-managed or will there be varying degrees of autonomy? Will the management reside within predetermined units or across a body of individuals who dynamically form their own project teams as needed? Will there be greatly reduced levels of managers? Or, as at Morning Star, will there be no managers of others at all? Who, precisely, will be answerable to whom?

Many considerations will help you to resolve these questions and others like them. And, as we have said, some of those considerations will be personal and philosophical. For instance, as a company leader, to what extent do you believe in personal freedom or the right of those in the workplace to be happy?

Which Path for You? (Hint: There is no "right" answer)

All of the considerations mentioned previously will be part of the self-assessment process we'll be describing in the following chapter, and they were essential to the decisions made by leaders of other self-managed or future-looking companies, too. In a moment, we'll take a look at some of those companies, and the governance frameworks they chose to deploy. Whether or not they were familiar with organizational framework terms such as *teleocracy* or *holacracy* at the time of their own assessments, they still may have opted for a form of autonomous or semi-autonomous governance that resembles one of those frameworks or others like them. Or they may have opted for the simplicity of true self-management.

As business moves deeper into the twenty-first century, organizations can and will take many paths to more vibrant, engaging, free, sustainable, respectful, and high-performing work environments that rely on individual choice, commitment, and fulfillment—not coercion. Today, organizing options include holacracy, teleocracy, sociocracy, workplace democracy, wirearchy, podularity, self-management, ROWE (Results Only Work Environment), agile management, horizontal management, wiki management, radical management, lattice management, and any number of approaches that shift the bureaucratic focus back to the effectiveness of individuals. Below is a sampling of such approaches; I have included references to companies relying on them, where applicable. The selection is meant to represent a core sample of rubrics, theories, frameworks, methods, concepts, systems, and approaches and is not intended to be exhaustive or complete.

HOLACRACY

According to HolacracyOne, Holacracy "brings structure and discipline to a peer-to-peer workplace."[33] Launched in 2007 by management thinkers and entrepreneurs Brian Robertson and Tom Thomison, Holacracy is a self-management framework that invites everyone in an organization to participate in governance, role-based decision-making, and shared purpose. It is designed to replace the obsolete predict-and-control paradigm with an adaptive, twenty-first century approach of sense-and-respond.

---

33   "What is Holacracy," Holacracy, accessed January 17, 2019, https://www.holacracy.org/
      what-is-holacracy?hilite=%27brings%27%2C%27structure%27%2C%27and%27%2C%27disci
      pline%27%2C%27peer-to-peer%27%2C%27workplace%27.

In 2013, Zappos CEO Tony Hsieh adopted this structure for his 1,500 employees. His aim was to create an enterprise that was less like a hierarchical, bureaucratic corporation, and more like a "city" in which people and businesses self-organize. *The Wall Street Journal* has reported that more than 300 companies have experimented with Holacracy in the past decade.[34]

HOLACRACY

Image created by Mohammed Ali Vakil with Calm Achiever, a certified Holacracy Provider, and used with permission of Brian J. Robertson of HolacracyOne, LLC and Mohammed Ali Vakil.

---

34 Rachel Emma Silverman, "5 Things on Having No Boss," *The Wall Street Journal*, May 20, 2015, https://blogs.wsj.com/briefly/2015/05/20/5-things-on-having-no-boss/.

DEMOCRACY

Organizational democracy is a movement promoted by the WorldBlu organization, which is headed by founder Traci Fenton.

According to the website, WorldBlu: Freedom at Work, organizational democracy is a "system of organization that is based on freedom, instead of fear and control. It's a way of designing organizations to amplify the possibilities of human potential—and the organization as a whole." WorldBlu is driven by an audacious vision to have one billion people working in freedom around the world. A list of ten principles (described in greater detail on the WorldBlu website) defines the democratic workplace:

1. Purpose and Vision

2. Transparency

3. Dialogue and Listening

4. Fairness and Dignity

5. Accountability

6. Individual and Collective

7. Choice

8. Integrity

9. Decentralization

10. Reflection and Evaluation

Equipped with these principles, WorldBlu maintains scorecards that evaluate the overall design of an organization along a fear-based to freedom-centered continuum in three core areas: leadership, individual performance, and systems and processes. In that way, the progress of participating companies can be measured as they evolve along the continuum. To date, those companies include Davita Healthcare Partners, DreamHost, the WD-40 Company, and PropellerNet. But the WorldBlu organization boasts a diverse roster of companies around the globe, in industries including technology, manufacturing, health care, education, retail, and professional services. For more information about democracy in the workplace, read *The Democratic Enterprise: Liberating your Business with Freedom, Flexibility and Commitment* by Lynda Gratton.[35]

TELEOCRACY

A key advocate for teleocracy as an organizational framework is author and consultant Dean Tucker, an engineer and Boeing veteran of NASA's Project Apollo and Boeing's 747 jetliner.

Teleocracy (derived from the Greek term *teleos*, meaning "purpose") is a management framework based on a sense of clear purpose—especially important to millennials who, as we have discussed, are not interested in remaining blindly loyal to a company for untold years, as were their parents. Millennials seek work/life balance and do not fear job loss; they need to be engaged by being instilled with a sense of company purpose and meaning that is connected to the larger world. Teleocracy—or "purpose-driven management"—aims to address that need via purpose, values, and vision statements that are then fulfilled through self-organizing teams. Other teleocracy features are:

- **Open book management** (where employees can read and understand financial statements and see the impact of their activities on the bottom line).

---

35   Lynda Gratton, *The Democratic Enterprise: Liberating your Business with Freedom, Flexibility and Commitment* (New Jersey: FT Press, 2004).

- **Employees as a high-priority class** of enterprise stakeholders.

- **Novel compensation schemas.**

- **Statistically sound, time-based performance measures** that trigger conversations where employees are free to tell each other the truth.

For more on teleocracy, read Tucker's *Using the Power of Purpose: How to Overcome Bureaucracy and Achieve Extraordinary Business Success,*[36] which details seventy-plus examples of "purpose-driven companies whose stock outperforms their peer companies by six to one."

SOCIOCRACY

A key advocate for sociocracy is John Buck, a thoughtful, inquisitive proponent of sociocracy in organizations. His consultancy promotes "responsive, effective, adaptive, transparent organizations." The group offers training, facilitation, sociocracy implementation, and mentoring services. Promised outcomes include improved capacity, better results, greater harmony, reduced overhead, distributed authority, and a focus on work that matters.

Sociocracy isn't new: the first sociocratic organization was founded in 1926 by Kees Boeke and his wife, Betty Cadbury, both educators in the Netherlands where they started a school based on sociocratic consent principles that still operates today. John Buck and Sharon Villines released their seminal work on sociocracy in 2007. The heart of sociocracy is rooted in three principles:

---

36   Dean Tucker, *Using the Power of Purpose: How to Overcome Bureaucracy and Achieve Extraordinary Business Success* (Bloomington, Indiana: AuthorHouse, 2008).

- **Consent**—the corridor through which all policy decisions must pass.

- **Circles**—semi-autonomous organs within the overall organizational structure. Circles use consent-based decision processes to establish policies within their domain of responsibility. Distributed leadership ensures that everyone affected by a decision has a voice.

- **Double-linking**—establishing feedback loops between circles (nuances of double-linking can be explored on the organization's website).

The principles are supported by "apps," which include transparent elections of individuals to roles within circles, membership (adding or removing members of circles), and performance reviews of circle members by fellow circle members. Their clients include manufacturers, trade associations, residential care providers, schools and nonprofits. For more on sociocracy, read *We the People: Consenting to a Deeper Democracy* by John Buck and Sharon Villines.[37]

A state-of-the-art version, Sociocracy 3.0, was launched as an open-source framework by James Priest and Bernhard Bockelbrink in 2015. According to their website, they "seek to make S3 available and applicable to as many organizations as possible and provide resources under a Creative Commons Free Culture License for people who want to learn, apply and tell others about Sociocracy 3.0."[38] Priest and Bockelbrink, along with team member Liliana David, created *Sociocracy 3.0—A Practical Guide* (available on their website).

---

37 John Buck and Sharon Villines, *We the People: Consenting to a Deeper Democracy* (Sociocracy.info, 2007).

38 Berhard Brockelbrink, James Priest, and Liliana David, "History of Sociocracy 3.0," Sociocracy 3.0, 2007, https://sociocracy30.org/the-details/history/.

WIREARCHY

Wirearchy is a concept launched in 1999 by lifelong social architect Jon Husband. The movement's website stresses that, though it may sound like one, wirearchy is not a technology paradigm, but rather "a dynamic two-way flow of power and authority based on knowledge, trust, credibility and a focus on results, enabled by interconnected people and technology."

Wirearchy emerged as an organizing principle generated by the now-interconnected information flows of the twenty-first century. It "informs the ways that purposeful human activities and the structures in which they are contained are evolving from top-down direction and supervision (hierarchy's *command-and-control*) to *champion-and-channel.*" The concept makes possible the "*championing* of ideas and innovation, and the *channeling* of time, energy, authority and resources to testing those ideas and the possibilities for innovation carried in those ideas."[39]

Here again, principles are used to define and design purpose, context, and the way things are intended to operate within a given company or organization. *Wirearchy: Sketches for the Future of Work* is a helpful, multi-authored e-book of thoughts, guidance, and concepts that relate to wirearchy in the workplace.[40] Husband is in good company with notable contributors, such as digital workplace researcher and author, Jane McConnell (*The Organization in the Digital Age)*; management trend-spotter, Thierry de Baillon; ex-investment banker now author and blogger, Rob Paterson; chairman of the internet Time Alliance thinktank, Harold Jarche; and social/organizational network analysis expert, Valdis Krebs, among others.

---

39   Jon Husband, "What is Wirearchy?," LinkedIn, November 24, 2014, https://www.linkedin.com/pulse/20141124231801-69412-what-is-wirearchy/.

40   The Wirearchy Commons, *Wirearchy: Sketches for the Future of Work* (Wirearchy, 2015).

Below is a sketch of hierarchy vs. wirearchy, from one of Husband's own blog entries. It may be simple, but, next to hierarchy's pyramid architecture it clearly demonstrates wirearchy's unstructured, dynamic flow (or "channeling") of power and authority that enables the "championing" of ideas and innovation everywhere within an organization. Conversely, note how in hierarchy, innovation is often driven *outside* the organizational pyramid. As Husband observes: "These 'new' hyperlinked conditions have made all kinds of information and knowledge accessible to us almost immediately. They have also made it easy to share, examine, and use pertinent information and knowledge in context. These 'new' conditions are not going away. They will intensify and engage us more and more frequently. The need for unlearning, continuous learning, and adaptability in pursuit of high performance has never been more real nor more critical."

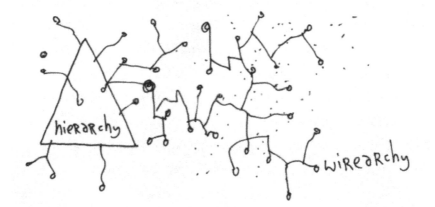

Wirearchy's unstructured, dynamic flow of authority enables championing of ideas from everywhere in the enterprise. © Copyright Jon Husband.

PODULARITY

Podularity has been around in one incarnation or other since at least the late 1980s when Volvo moved car assembly in some of its plants from the assembly line to small team units of workers (in effect, pods) wholly responsible for assembling Volvos, car by car. The idea was to boost sales and positively impact quality by relying on independent, invested pods of collaborating individuals to see a vehicle through from start to finish. It was hoped that this approach would be more effective than expecting workers' anonymous contributions as part of the larger whole, the corporation, to take quality and innovation to the next level. Quality and productivity took off.

Companies such as Kyocera, the tech-device maker; Nordstrom, the apparel retailer; and Valve Corporation, an entertainment and software technology producer, have utilized podularity in one fashion or another. A *podular organization,* however, ditches the traditional top-down, divisional "silo" organizational structure for pods in which each role of the company is represented and every unit is autonomous; a fractal representation of the entire business. Pods, say their advocates, allow a company to deliver greater value to customers without disrupting other business activities or triggering disparate support activities. Pods focus on holistic goals for their customers and the company rather than simply carrying out steps or stages. If a single pod falters, the whole can still thrive.

The goal of podularity is to reduce interdependency and yet boost coordination and distribution of the work load across the enterprise. Still, there are varying methods of connecting the pods to the larger business; some proponents favor net-like scenarios; others suggest hub-and-spoke, multiple hub-and-spoke, or even linear connection schemes. Some organizations have gone wholly podular, while others utilize podular frameworks for only certain areas of the company—

such as on the assembly floor of an auto manufacturing plant. Yet whether it's an intricate, formalized structure of circles-within-circles (holacracy), or a dynamically, organically forming and reforming non-structure of agile, self-determining groups (self-management), podularity is now a widely embraced concept. Below are illustrations of both a pod and a podular organization configuration—of which there are many.

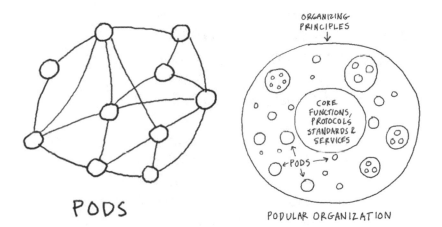

The single pod (left) is a self-sustaining "organism" within one example of a configuration of pods (right). "Pods" and "Podular Organization" by Dave Gray is licensed under CC BY-ND 2.0. https://creativecommons.org/licenses/by-nd/2.0/.

DELIBERATELY DEVELOPMENTAL ORGANIZATIONS

The idea of a Deliberately Developmental Organization (DDO) was espoused by authors Robert Kegan and Lisa Laskow Lahey (with contributors Matthew L. Miller, Andy Fleming, and Deborah Helsing) in their 2016 book, *An Everyone Culture: Becoming a Deliberately Developmental Organization.*[41] In it, the writers describe the need for organizations to align with everyone's inner goal: to grow. Making

---

41   Robert Kegan and Lisa Laskow Lahey, *An Everyone Culture: Becoming a Deliberately Developmental Organization* (Brighton: Harvard Business Review Press, 2016).

growth opportunities available to everyone in an organization—not just "high potentials"—creates a path to realizing unused potential.

The authors share cases studies, stories, and practices that effectively communicate the benefits of embracing DDO principles. While not an approach to organizational structure per se, the DDO concept is about unleashing the human potential in every person within the organization.

JAIPUR RUGS: SELF-MANAGED ART THAT YOU CAN WALK ON

"We Don't Sell Carpets; We Sell a Family's Blessing"

Nand Kishore Chaudhary, known to his close colleagues as NKC, is a man on a mission. The humble founder of Jaipur Rugs, now employing 40,000 weavers making hand-knotted decorative rugs for sale in forty countries, is theorizing how to elevate the collaborative and decision-making powers of the workforce using the power of organizational self-management. He, and his company, have come a long way since starting up in 1978 on 5,000 rupees borrowed from his father after walking away from a stable banker's job to pursue his entrepreneurial dreams.

Riding around on a scooter, he started making carpets for sale with nine weavers working two looms. Over the next three years, he expanded the number of looms to ten, requiring many more artisans to operate them. The media began to pay attention: art historian Ilay Cooper wrote a 1980 feature story on NKC and Jaipur Rugs for *Inside-Outside* magazine. The media attention made sense: gorgeous, premium-quality, hand-woven carpets are fine art that you can walk on (or hang on the wall), and last for generations to come.

A strategy began to take shape in NKC's mind: eliminate the exploitative middlemen who take profits out of the system and steer those profits directly to the amazing artisan weavers who create the art in the first place: the villagers from the untouchable class who do the actual work. Global markets were thrilled to make the walkable tapestries available for customers willing to pay premium prices—and Jaipur Rugs was ready to supply them.

Growing demand for the beautiful artisanal rug patterns dreamed up by Jaipur Rugs' inspired design team led to expanded production in India's rural zones, using walkie-talkies (a rarely permitted privilege of the Indian government at the time) to manage the supply chain. In the late 1990's, Jaipur expanded to include a US sales and distribution arm. The company's weaver community expanded rapidly to fulfill global demand, with weavers from Rajasthan villages and Gujarat tribal areas skillfully producing wondrous creations to delight the senses of touch and sight.

While developing his bottom-up business strategy, NKC's daughter Kavita ("Kavi") Chaudhary undertook professional studies and achieved design excellence, launching collections and winning international design awards. One of her collections, Anthar (meaning "differences"), is a family of rugs born of error (hence the label "Error Collection"). Perfectly knotted or not (no pun intended), every carpet tells a story. One of the famous carpets from the Error Collection tells the story of three weavers who didn't get along that well in the beginning (at the bottom of the carpet, where it all starts)—and their disjointed weave shows it. As the three weavers got to know each other better, they began collaborating at a higher level, and their weaves got tighter and more coordinated. Finally, at the top of the carpet, the team artistry shines as the weavers are working harmoniously together in trusting, perfect synchronicity. A carpet thus became both a metaphor for teamwork and excellence. By learning how to work together, the three weavers overcame their differences.

As Kavi sagely observed, "Anthar speaks to our goal of connecting the world from the smallest villages in India to the top cities of the globe using design as a medium. What normally would have been thought of as a mistake has transformed into a piece of art."[42] In a recent video interview, she stated it simply: "Beauty to me is about being in harmony."[43] Anthar won a German Design Award in 2016.

One of NKC's ambitions is to connect the weavers directly to the customers. Initiatives like sending handcrafted postcards from weavers to customers and taking weavers to international award events are two ways that artisans connect personally with the marketplace. The personal connection is crucial: as NKC says, "We don't sell carpets; we sell a family's blessing."[44] That's almost unique in the world, and an amazing testament to the humble founder of Jaipur Rugs and his own extraordinarily talented family. Customers, feeling blessed by the beauty of their rugs, often visit the villages in which their rugs were made to meet and personally thank the creators—a virtuous

---

42 "Anthar, the carpet by Jaipur Rugs of its Project Error collection, when an error becomes a work of art," Infurma, November 30, 2015, https://news.infurma.es/decoration-2/anthar-the-carpet-by-jaipur-rugs-of-its-project-error-collection-when-an-error-becomes-a-work-of-art/12945.

43 "The Jaipur Story," Jaipur Rugs Company, April 26, 2016, video, https://www.youtube.com/watch?v=EAAGyCjsUWk.

44 James Allen, "Jaipur Rugs: Selling a Family's Blessing, Bain & Company, April 8, 2015, https://www.bain.com/insights/jaipur-rugs-selling-a-familys-blessing-fm-blog2/.

cycle of artistry, generosity and kindness (and a lot of work—a single rug may contain a million knots).

Connecting the weavers with the customers has been a huge catalyst for human development. Periodically bringing the weavers together to see the finished product has led to greater engagement and innovation. A new program to allow weavers to develop their own designs has unlocked creative genius and innovation. Weavers are now sharing aspects of their own lives and telling their own stories through their art. As Kavi notes, "Through the rugs, the customer has an insight into the weaver's life."[45] The villages, the animals, the people and the landscapes all become part of the artistic story that customers value. The circle connecting weaver to customer and back to weaver is paying untold dividends of happiness.

NKC's idea was, and is, to improve lives through personal, economic, educational, and social empowerment rather than just giving away charity.[46] As he told me on a recent visit: "The weavers are making better lives for themselves. They can now provide educations for their children, make it possible for their husbands to leave the village to work, and to better their communities." His business goal is personal development, economic self-determination, and prosperity for all.[47] Through it all, he remains humble: "I never say that I have done any good to the weavers. It is just the opposite: They have done good to me."[48]

45   "Jaipur Rugs: Founder's Mentality in Action," bainandcompany, May 7, 2016, video, https://www.youtube.com/watch?v=jPEY1KRYf3E.
46   "Weaver," nkchaudhary, accessed May 2, 2019, http://www.nkchaudhary.com/weaver/.
47   Ibid.
48   Anshul Dhamija, "Jaipur Rugs' Nand Kishore Chaudhary: A rugs to riches story," *Forbes India*, January 16, 2018, http://www.forbesindia.com/article/social-impact-special-2017/jaipur-rugs-nand-kishore-chaudhary-a-rugs-to-riches-story/49135/1.

That sounds like the epitome of sound social entrepreneurship.

But NKC isn't done yet—not by a long shot.

Enterprise Self-Management: Unlocking Unlimited Potential

As the company grew, NKC found himself consumed with running an international business and not spending as much time on the front line as he wished, thus losing touch with the people he loved—the weavers. He launched a series of initiatives to get back to his original love: initiatives in education, literacy, coaching, mentoring, engagement, and organizational self-management. As NKC spent time reconnecting with the weavers, vast opportunities emerged. He realized that, as Jaipur Rugs manager Sanjay Singh observed, "They are not only weavers. They have wonderful qualities within them. Some of them are wonderful mobilizers, quality controllers, teachers."[49] Might NKC's great experiment hold a key to implementing self-management at scale?

I was privileged to visit one of the villages and hear from the leaders responsible for the transformation, and from the weavers making it happen.

If self-management is about anything, it's about respecting the voices of each and every member of an organization. NKC embodies a deep-seated belief in the dignity of every individual in his self-management journey. He created an amazing community of weavers by disregarding India's rigid caste system, not believing that human beings should be "untouchable." He believes that people should not be judged by caste,

---

49   "Jaipur Rugs: Founder's Mentality in Action," bainandcompany, May 7, 2016, video, https://www.youtube.com/watch?v=jPEY1KRYf3E.

but by their own deeds. He finds beauty wherever he goes, in everyone he meets, in everything he sees.

As I toured a village with NKC; his daughter, Kavi; and HR leader, Amit Kumar Agarwal, the weavers presented themselves as a living testament to the power of NKC's self-management vision. We heard from quality leader Harfool about the importance of listening to the weavers, teaching them with patience and kindness, and helping them improve their lives. We heard from Swati, who is coaching and mentoring weavers in their new roles as self-managed leaders and innovators, involved in product development and design. And we heard from the weavers themselves, who are gaining dignity, self-worth, and a future in their new self-managed ecosystem.

The basic repetitive movement: openly listen, teach, mentor, and release is now bringing self-managed dignity to thousands in rural India—and paying dividends for Jaipur Rugs. NKC's statement to me about the power of self-management, even in the people of the "untouchable" class: "Don't tell me that these people can't manage themselves. They've already learned how to survive."

Even as he unlocks the limitless human potential of the weavers, NKC faces a new challenge: how to develop deep humility and appreciation for others among the educated professionals he hired to run the rapidly growing business. His philosophy of life is *finding yourself through losing yourself*.[50] It's a process of becoming selfless, losing attachment to ego, and embracing simplicity and love. How can he get his professional managers to surrender to a purpose larger than themselves? That challenge represents the next

---

50 "Philosophy," nkchaudhary, accessed May 2, 2019, http://www.nkchaudhary.com/philosophy/.

frontier of organizational self-management Jaipur Rugs and its remarkable founder.

An Entire Global Enterprise Built on Love

Kahlil Gibran said that work is love made visible.

James Allen, in a Bain & Company blog titled "Jaipur Rugs: Selling a Family's Blessing,"[51] told a prescient story about NKC's university days:

> The professor was asking about the purpose of business. One by one, students raised their hands to offer views, and you can imagine the answers: shareholder value creation, serving customers, beating the competition, and so on. Mr. Chaudhary raised his hand to speak, telling the class, "Business is next to love. It is the creator and preserver of a civilization." His teacher commented to the class, "This, ladies and gentlemen, is a successful business entrepreneur."

Talking about his relationship with the weavers, NKC declared: "I love them so much."

Jaipur Rugs is an entire global business built on love, one knot at a time, with a visionary founder's dream for a self-managed future clearly in sight.

ROWE (RESULTS-ONLY WORK ENVIRONMENT)

Jody Thompson and Cali Ressler developed the concept of the Result-Only Work Environment (ROWE), establishing it in electronics retailer Best Buy in 2005, with impressive results. (Best Buy

---

51 James Allen, "Jaipur Rugs: Selling a Family's Blessing, Bain & Company, April 8, 2015, https://www.bain.com/insights/jaipur-rugs-selling-a-familys-blessing-fm-blog2/.

has since abandoned the effort, despite saving $2.2 million over three years, according to a 2013 article by Monique Valcour in the *Harvard Business Review*).[52] The purpose of ROWE is to provide employees 100 percent autonomy regarding how they perform work, while maintaining 100 percent accountability for results. ROWE has been implemented in more than forty companies.

The conceptual foundation of ROWE is the well-documented recognition that people desire autonomy at work while needing feedback on performance. Thompson and Ressler's book on their approach is *Why Work Sucks and How to Fix It: The Results-Only Revolution*.[53]

HORIZONTAL MANAGEMENT

Mario Kaphan is the founder of Vagas, a Brazilian recruitment software company based in São Paulo, Brazil. Vagas is the country's leading recruitment software company with 2,400 clients, including sixty-five of Brazil's one hundred largest companies. The company refers to its system as "horizontal management," and created an environment of no command authority. According to the Management Innovation Exchange website,[54] the VAGAS ecosystem receives an average of 300,000 unique visitors daily. Additionally, vagas.com.br ranks among the 200 largest sites in Brazil (6,000 worldwide). The site is one of the leading Brazilian recruitment sites, and more than 90 percent of all visits are organic, that is, not originating from paid advertising or similar.

---

52   Monique Valcour, "The End of 'Results Only' at Best Buy Is Bad News," *Harvard Business Review*, March 8, 2013, https://hbr.org/2013/03/goodbye-to-flexible-work-at-be.
53   Jody Thompson and Cali Ressler, *Why Work Sucks and How to Fix It: The Results-Only Revolution* (New York: Portfolio, 2008).
54   www.managementexchange.com

ORGANIZATIONAL SELF-MANAGEMENT

Launched in 1990 by entrepreneur Chris Rufer, The Morning Star Company was one of the first wholly self-managed organizations in the US. It is now the world's largest tomato processor. Morning Star became a model for dynamic, self-perpetuating informal workplace structure. Importantly, self-management is based on life principles that are evident everywhere, and are fundamental to its success:

- People are generally happier when they have control over their own life (and work).

- Decision-making authority is most effective when it is closest to the actual locus of any work.

- People tend to flourish with greater responsibility.

- Bureaucratic hierarchies spawn the need for ever-increasing management and control; bureaucracy does not scale, and is ultimately self-defeating.

- Worldwide, in government or business, freedom tends to engender economic prosperity, while repression generally breeds corruption.

- Forming the basis of successful self-management are two primary tenets:

  1. No one should be coerced to do anything.

  2. People should keep their commitments (everyone is responsible and accountable to everyone else in the organization).

The illustration below shows how colleagues at the Morning Star Company collaborate with and are accountable to other colleagues within the company, just as in their everyday lives.

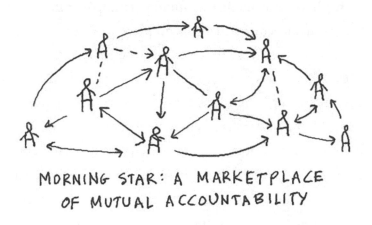

MORNING STAR: A MARKETPLACE
OF MUTUAL ACCOUNTABILITY

"Morning Star: A Marketplace of Mutual Accountability" by Dave Gray
is licensed under CC BY-ND 2.0. https://creativecommons.org/licenses/by-nd/2.0/.

Self-management is simple and natural; it represents the way we manage our lives daily in the world at large. Examples of companies that have either deployed self-management or hold true self-management as their end-model are The Morning Star Company, Fresh Fill, Sudwerk Brewing, and Apollo Education Group (one business unit).

Self-Management by Degrees vs. Pure Self-Management

As a member of the Morning Star launch team, I can tell you that the process of creating a wholly self-managed organization from the ground up was challenging but, ultimately, extraordinarily rewarding. It required that we not just consider the significant bottom-line benefits to the company of greater innovation and accountability in the workplace, but also the untold benefits of work/life integration for all the members of an organization, and the resulting contribution to society at large.

As we have seen in the continuum examples throughout this chapter, self-management in the workplace can take many forms, and some of its practices are widespread: self-directed work teams, employee autonomy or empowerment, distributed decision-making, and "flattening" the organization by eliminating bureaucratic obstacles and unnecessary layers of management.

It's important to note that in a purely self-managed enterprise, "structure" arises spontaneously—that is, *no* organizational structure is imposed on the members of the company. (If colleagues in a self-managed environment want to voluntarily associate in a mini-hierarchy for purposes of decision-making or work direction, that's perfectly fine—as long as the association is a voluntary one, not imposed by force, and is subject to voluntary *disassociation* by the parties involved.) Those who work within the company are responsible for organizing their own relationships and are guided by their "personal commercial mission" (what they are challenged to achieve for the enterprise), just as they are guided by their daily missions in their everyday lives. The commercial mission, then, becomes their real "boss," although it is fair to say that their colleagues across the enterprise are their bosses, too, with respect to individual commitments.

And what of the managerial functions of planning, organizing, staffing, directing, and controlling, which may previously have resided within layers of corporate management? In the purest form of self-management, all managerial functions, too, become the personal responsibility of each member of the organization, as groups of peers come together to achieve a particular goal and, thus, plan, hire, direct, and control any given project as needed. In a wholly self-managed organization, no circles or pods are designated or assigned; groups come together, produce, disband, and re-form organically, as required. No complex charts of pyramids, or diagrams of circles, pods, or networks dictate the way that peers within the organization organize. They organize naturally.

Pure self-management, then, is not employee "empowerment" bestowed by others. With all members of the organization personally responsible for building their own working relationships, planning their own work, coordinating that work with others, and acquiring needed resources and managing staffing, the need for *any* formal hierarchy is completely eliminated and the self-management process becomes self-perpetuating. Self-management is beyond empowerment. Self-management is power itself.

Self-management is beyond empowerment. Self-management is power itself.

How Do Companies Decide Which Model to Adopt?

The reality is, there are any number of ways to hone in on a model of self-management that is best-suited to an enterprise, and no way is right or wrong. Often, the driver of organizational change (usually the CEO or company head, but sometimes another member of senior management) will start reading about one new model and then either move on to other models, comparing and contrasting, or else dive deeper into a single model, reading everything available that is pertinent. I am frequently called in to acquaint a company leader with the concept and workings of self-management because he or she will have read a book or article or heard a speaker on the topic. That doesn't necessarily mean that the company is only considering the form of natural, organically dynamic self-management within which

I worked; the leadership team may, in fact, be meeting with consultants representing any number of organizational models. Or not.

Zappos CEO Tony Hsieh, for instance, was impressed by Brian Robertson's holacracy model. With no fear of experimentation in his company's already vibrant culture, Hsieh became the most significant adopter of circles-within-circles restructuring governance and technology.

Company heads often send their leadership teams to conferences, meetings, and seminars where they can meet organizational model creators or those spearheading movements. The teams return with a wealth of feedback not only from the movement leaders, but also, importantly, from client companies and others currently in the process of rolling out the new organizational structures (or nonstructures, as is the case with pure self-management).

And then there are the uber-visionary leaders whose personal lives and missions so perfectly intersect with their business philosophies that self-management is the natural outcome. I recently reconnected with just such an individual: Brian Rocha, CEO of Fresh Fill in Los Banos, California. Brian and his partner, Brett Windecker, had spoken with me eighteen months earlier, before they began hiring for their new venture. From their earliest discussions about their venture, they had known that the simple, holistic form of organically self-organizing self-management (on the Morning Star end of the spectrum) was the only model for their new convenience-store company. After our initial talks about self-management, I found myself stepping in again, many months later, to help guide them through the hiring process, but they had needed little in the way of convincing or consulting before they began their own concerted organizational development work, modeled after Morning Star.

Other company heads are not so lucky. They lead more conventional, bureaucratically entrenched organizations and, for one or more compelling reasons, have come to realize that their companies must undergo organizational retooling or suffer serious consequences. No matter which model they choose, these CEOs and their leadership teams often have the most difficult route to self-management, for the concept may feel alien to them, even as they perceive its value. These company leaders, especially, need time to read, discuss, tour, and meet with various model proponents. In that way, they can not only familiarize themselves with self-management but, crucially, they can conduct a thoughtful and multifaceted self-assessment of business and personal values. Only then will they be able to determine where in the continuum of organizational self-management their enterprise should comfortably and successfully land.

CHAPTER 6

DETERMINING WHERE YOUR ORGANIZATION FITS IN THE SELF-MANAGEMENT CONTINUUM

For a long time, we thought the world operated based on Newtonian principles. We didn't know better and thought we needed to interfere with the life's self-organizing urge and try to control one another.

—FRÉDÉRIC LALOUX, AUTHOR OF
REINVENTING ORGANIZATIONS

EX-MCKINSEY & COMPANY management consultant Frédéric Laloux, quoted above, also remarked: "The principal science of the next century will be the study of complex, autocatalytic, self-organizing, nonlinear, and adaptive systems." In other words: *self-management.*

In the previous chapter, we saw that there are now a growing number of company leaders who believe that some form of self-management is a better (and inevitable) route to a happy, inspired, engaged, and innovative workforce. These company owners and CEOs may have opted for various *routes* to self-management, yet all undoubtedly saw self-organizing, nonlinear, and adaptive systems as core to the future success of their businesses—and key to a better world for all. Still, before these company leaders could embark on a route to transformative change within their organizations, each (formally or informally) earnestly assessed the current state of their organizations and company cultures, their own business and personal philosophies, and their visions for the future of their company. Without that pre-assessment process, a roadmap to any form of self-management could not be developed. What's more, without an initial self-assessment process, there is no way to determine precisely where on the continuum between rigid bureaucracy and full-blown self-management your own organization should reside.

Assessing Company Culture

Whether intentionally nurtured or not, all business enterprises have a culture. The culture is the embodiment of stereotypes and assumptions about how things should be done. It is tacit; it flows beneath the level of conscious awareness even as it guides actions and behaviors.[55] And it is powerful, like the current in a stream that guides everything in one direction.

Because most traditional company cultures are rooted in traditional management systems, the people within those companies align their expectations, behaviors, and activities around conventional expectations. They are guided by, "What does my boss think?" and, "How am I going to please or impress my boss and get ahead

---

55   Edgar Schein, *Corporate Culture Survival Guide* (San Francisco: Jossey-Bass Publishing, 2009).

in the organization?" Those values create one kind of culture: a command-and-control culture that most of us know well, for it has been pervasive for decades.

A self-managed organization has a culture vastly different from that of a traditional organization. A self-managed culture is driven by all of its members organizing around the questions, "What is the mission of the enterprise, and how do I align my purpose with it?" and, "How do I define my meaning and purpose in the organization by my actions and my behaviors around the pursuit of the mission?"

The culture of those who work within a self-managed enterprise then becomes one of, "How do I provide value for everyone around me?" That is because *anyone* in the self-managed organization—not solely a "boss"—can impact another individual's ability to fulfill his own purpose toward the company's mission. In a self-managed culture, the overall mission of the enterprise naturally becomes the North Star that guides the culture. All of the stakeholders know that they must provide value to everyone else around them in the enterprise, if they are also to provide value to the company's customers.

The culture of those who work within a self-managed enterprise then becomes one of, "How do I provide value for everyone around me?"

In a command-and-control culture, however, layers and layers of management have likely been tacked on through the years. The company culture is teeming with individuals who are concerned with impressing the boss, getting ahead, or making their own mark within the organization. The enterprise tenets might originally have been focused on the company's mission to create value for its customers, but that mission has become obscured by the command-and-control culture itself. Company leaders may wonder: How much house cleaning will it take to once again see our North Star and be guided by it?

Holistic Assessment: Balancing the Well-Being of All Stakeholders

For an organizational assessment to be valid and effective, it must take into account a holistic view. Does the current enterprise embrace the well-being of *all* stakeholders, not just customers? And does the vision of the future organization embrace a *holistic* viewpoint regarding stakeholders?

A stakeholder is any individual or any entity affected by the enterprise. That means: suppliers, customers, regulators, the community at large, the environment, employees, neighbors—every conceivable participant. In a successful enterprise, each stakeholder is equally important. Not sure you accept that notion? Look at it this way: In a more conventional enterprise, the focus is most often on one or two stakeholders. The mantra is, "Make the customer king!" or, "Employees are our greatest asset!" Yet, a holistic attitude that embraces and balances the well-being of all stakeholders is not simply about respecting the yin and yang of the natural world in which everything, ultimately, is complementary, interconnected, and interdependent. Self-management also recognizes that the balancing of stakeholders represents a powerful tool that can mean a real competitive edge over conventional business approaches.

Morning Star, for instance, sees the effective balancing of all stakeholders as a "dynamic adventure," helping the entire organization to keep driving profit. In fact, this stakeholder-balancing adventure is so vital to the Morning Star culture and the success of the enterprise that it is used as a gaming tool. In gaming mode, Morning Star colleagues routinely watch, assess, evaluate, and even emulate or create scenarios of stakeholder behaviors and indicators, looking for ways to proactively meet needs or attend to problems that may arise. No one can ever know for sure what will happen next in life or business, but to view the unknown as an adventure worthy of gaming puts a whole new spin on the *business* of business.

For Morning Star, balancing stakeholder needs can provide an unparalleled competitive edge while delivering genuine value to stakeholders. In essence, it allows the company to be a true No-Limits Enterprise, driving profit through multiple channels. Profit is simply the difference between the value you *create* for the world, versus the value you *consume* in creating products or services for the world. It's like the applause you get from a theater full of play-goers when you have given them more delight than any discomfort they may have experienced parting with the dollars for their tickets.

Yet, to managers and even senior leadership in more conventional businesses, moving to the holistic stakeholder approach of self-management can be anxiety provoking because it flies in the face of command-and-control. These individuals have risen through the ranks and acquired perks and power along the way. To them, the concept of balancing stakeholder needs may even be alarming.

Not too long ago, when I was teaching a self-management course to a couple dozen executives whose company was moving away from its traditional organizational structure, one executive suddenly stood up and blurted out, "What's going to happen to *me*?" His peers told him to sit down and reassured him that he'd be fine. They added that he'd be making many of the same decisions, he just wouldn't be commanding the obedience of subordinates. I then pointed out that balancing all stakeholder needs not only enables a No-Limits

Enterprise, it makes possible a no-limits career, as a company that rises higher and higher elevates its workforce right along with it. I also explained that self-management actually *liberates* managers and leaders because, instead of constantly being charged with solving other people's problems, they can at last challenge their colleagues to first take a whack at those problems themselves. Self-managed leaders don't have to be the expert in every situation, and many feel freed (finally!) to refocus on skill sets they value most, rather than on people management—something for which they may not have initially signed on.

The truth is, everyone has self-interests. The challenge lies in incorporating self-interest into the creation of value for the world at large. For when you create value for the world, it comes back to benefit you. Self-interest is actually *served* by creating value for others. That's the dynamic of freedom.

The challenge lies in incorporating self-interest into the creation of value for the world at large. For when you create value for the world, it comes back to benefit you.

Yet, what about the loss of corporate power? Scientists now know that the human brain is physiologically affected by power. Power, as it happens, can be as physically addictive as a drug, and can be as difficult to give up. But replacing conventional modes of corporate power-mongering with the limitless power to drive advancement can go a long way to easing the transition to a new organizational model that balances the needs of all stakeholders. It's a paradox: limiting individual power over others unleashes an organization's collective power to achieve greatness.

Assessing Personal and Business Values

When a business leader sits down to examine his or her own personal views and how those private philosophies intersect with business values, interesting things happen. Fairly early in the process, most leaders come to acknowledge that a certain amount of caring for other human beings comes into play, no matter how competitive or bottom-line-driven the business goals are. That's because, as we pointed out earlier in Chapter 2 (Bureaucracy: 15 Unavoidable Challenges), all businesses are essentially about meeting any of the eight basic human needs, detailed here a bit more scientifically according to Maslow's Hierarchy of Needs:[56]

1. **Physiological** (food, warmth, shelter, sex, water)

2. **Safety** (all things relating to an orderly world where injustice is under control)

3. **Love and Belonging** (friendship, intimacy, a supportive family)

4. **Self-esteem** (engagement, recognition, contribution, acceptance)

5. **Cognitive needs** (learning, exploring, understanding the world around us)

6. **Aesthetic** (beauty, nature, art)

7. **Self-actualization** (making the most of our abilities, striving to be the best we can be)

8. **Self-transcendence** (spirituality and integrity)

---

56   Abraham Maslow, "A Theory of Human Motivation," *Psychological Review* 50 (1943): 370–396.

Even if you've never looked at it that way, your business is all about meeting one or more human needs in a manner that is satisfactory to people, so that they are willing to pay for your product or service and thus allow you to make a profit. Empirically speaking, you can't do that if you don't care about people. (You can certainly try, but eventually your endeavor will suffer as customers go elsewhere.) Work really *is* "love made visible."

All of this means that, as the leader of an organization, your personal views do indeed intersect with your business goals and, just as importantly, they should. Self-assessment, then, is your opportunity to examine your personal values and philosophies and align them with those of the business. For instance, do you believe that people are most productive when they are free to speak up? Innovate? Drive change? Do you believe that people work best when they organize and collaborate organically, as they do in their everyday lives? Do you believe that people who are *happy* at work tend to work more productively? Do you believe that human beings have free will?

SEMCO: RADICAL WITH A CONSCIENCE

In Brazil, Semco CEO Ricardo Semler believes that those who work for the company are as capable of determining a fair wage for their work as Human Resources people are; after all, they have access to all the same industry and company data. He also believes that Semco workers are perfectly able to determine, on a daily basis, how many hours they need to complete their work. Sometimes, that amounts to what would constitute overtime at another company. Sometimes, it means that for producing so efficiently, their reward is time away from the workplace during what would be normal working hours elsewhere. Semler has always believed that his workers are best equipped to determine what is needed to do their jobs, and that they are happier and more productive in what the press calls the company's "radically" self-managed environment. Applied to the reorganization of what originally was a bureaucratic family business, Semler's personal value system has worked well in tandem with the goals of the enterprise; growth has been exponential and contributions to the region, including much-needed schools, have garnered praise.

FRESH FILL: BETTER WORLD, BETTER BUSINESS

For the brand-new Fresh Fill[57] venture (launched January 2018 in Los Banos, CA), partners Brian Rocha and Brett Windecker knew from the onset that they would imbue their convenience-store enterprise with their personal "make the world a better place" standards in every way they could. No crowded aisles of beef jerky, stale donuts, chips, and sugar-laden sodas; no Twinkies, mediocre coffee, and dirty bathrooms. Yes, Fresh Fill patrons are the same road-weary customers who have been pit-stopping at typical American convenience stores for decades. Today, however, they pull up to a beautiful, solar-powered oasis with electric car-charging stations and sparkling clean bathrooms. Inside, wide-open gleaming white aisles offer healthy fruit and vegetable snacks; fresh, hot foods made with natural ingredients; a natural raw juice bar; a high-end, nitro-infused premium coffee machine; even a craft beer cave. There's kiosk ordering, a mobile app-only drive-through window, and more. Everything is kept scrupulously clean and well stocked by diligent workers who are managing themselves.

How does Fresh Fill do it? The secret is that the company attracts the best workers because it pays its workforce more than does its competition. Fresh Fill can afford to pay more because there is no

---

57   www.freshfillstores.com

designated management and, thus, none of the expensive "management tax" that goes along with layers of management, HR, and all the rest. At Fresh Fill, *every* worker is a manager. On the continuum of self-management, Fresh Fill is far to the right, alongside its Los Banos neighbor, Morning Star.

Personal mission development for staff is a priority at Fresh Fill, as is giving back to the Los Banos community in every way possible. (The store's grand opening was designed to churn proceeds right back into the community.) Rocha, Fresh Fill's founder, is a young, progressive globe trekker who was determined to bring all the enlightenment of his travels and third-world volunteer work back to the US. Rocha's forward-thinking entrepreneurial experience in the restaurant business and his expertise in organizational dynamics aligned perfectly with his personal value system.

It's clear that making the world a better place informed every decision the Fresh Fill partners made during their self-assessment process. (You can glimpse Brian Rocha's clearly conveyed personal value system at BrianRocha.com.) The two pondered long and hard, for instance, about the people whom Fresh Fill would hire: education level took a back seat to such qualities as passion, vision, "sharpness," and a willingness to work hard, communicate well, and make the world a better place for all. That kind of personal commitment is now bringing exceptional value to the Fresh Fill customer, true purpose and accountability to the Fresh Fill workforce, greater benefit and opportunity to the community, and—no small byproduct—an outstanding competitive edge to the Fresh Fill enterprise.

SELF-MANAGEMENT WITH A
CHANGING OF THE GUARD

A formidable commodity producer in the South (a client) has been thoroughly entrenched in conventional hierarchy for several years, but now things are ripe for change. With the recent installation of a new visionary CEO, this large company will seek to morph from bureaucracy to self-management. How did the decision for such radical change come about? In this case, the consensus-building effort was two-pronged: simultaneously from inside out and from outside in. The soon-to-be CEO knew that the company needed organizational change to forge ahead in the twenty-first century, and he was coming onboard to head up a leadership team already on his wavelength. Plans for a pilot implementation of self-management were already underway by time the new company head walked into his office for the first time.

In fact, there are many steps that companies often take in their earliest assessment processes, as they are considering a move to self-management. Some are as intangible as the one-way conversations that CEOs have "in their heads" as they mull over possibilities. Others are as tangible as a schedule of leadership team meetings for the purpose of open dialogue, or even anonymous electronic surveys of randomly chosen employees across the enterprise. Sometimes, simply reviewing a list of the exercises or issues that will initially be undertaken in the first stages of an organizational shift to self-management is enough to launch a serious self-assessment. Questions that frequently pop up are:

- **Will we be able to deconstruct what each of us does**, and reconstruct our purposes within our new organization?

- **Will we be able to—individually and in groups—create our own purpose statements** that align with our company mission?

- **Will we be able to identify which parts of "managing"** each of us will be personally responsible for?

- **What will be the scope** of each person's decision-making authority?

- **How will we measure performance** in our new self-managed enterprise?

It is questions such as these that sometimes expose the weak links that must be taken seriously. One leadership team I advised was determined to move to self-management until its members came to the decision-rights phase of their discussions. Conversations about surrendering conventional management power effectively harpooned any headway they had made previously. They were forced to abandon their organizational change when no one was willing to distribute decision-making authority.

Each company CEO and leadership team approaches the assessment process in a way that makes the most sense for them. The dedicated leadership team for the southern commodity producer I mentioned previously, for instance, opted for the following first steps for its own assessment process:

1. Site visits to self-managed companies.

2. Deep dialogue with subject matter experts.

3. Internal leadership assessment of risks and benefits.

4. Determination of site and timing for self-management experiments and a pilot project.

The team would tell you that the work they completed, even before their new leader arrived at headquarters, was crucial. All the initial and essential pieces were in place: a CEO actively driving positive change (albeit from offstage), a leadership team fully bought-in to the organizational change initiative, and an in-depth agenda to lay the groundwork for planning.

How different the situation has been for another client, a distributor of industrial equipment based in the Pacific Northwest. The CEO of that enterprise sees himself on a treadmill, watching bad decisions being made by managers despite elaborate controls and rigid authority structures. Initial assessment of the situation involved much soul-searching. His first personal self-assessment question: Did he even want to continue working in the business? Either way, he realized, he would need to find a way to fix the organization, so why not create a truly twenty-first-century workplace?

In this instance, we delivered an experiential masterclass that gave the leadership team a true sense of what it would be like to act as self-managers. Such enlightenment cannot come too early; it can inform many decisions to come, especially regarding precisely how far into self-management a company is disposed to move.

The masterclass immersion in the theory and practice of self-management can also lay the groundwork for an organization's key self-management principles, philosophies, and infrastructure. Exercises often include forming virtual companies and then walking people through the process of negotiating agreements that document continuous, ongoing, or recurrent commitments to peers plus the precise scope of each individual's decision-making authority. These exercises often flush out philosophical and practical questions or concerns that may not have risen to the surface previously. Such questions can be addressed in real time and may also impact the self-assessment process.

During the recent masterclass, for instance, one leadership team member expressed concern about factory safety in the absence of a bona fide boss watching over things. Wouldn't workers be tempted to take shortcuts that might result in harm to themselves or others? The question gave me an opportunity to point out that with accountable eyes everywhere, there is no inherent safety risk in organizational self-management. People will continue to be as safe as they choose to be (there's free will again). Yet think about it: Who is more likely to spot a safety issue in the workplace? A formal manager who wanders through a work area a number of times a day, or colleagues who are working side-by-side with their fellow colleagues all day long, and who have an affirmative obligation to speak up regarding any problem that enters their scope of awareness?

For the conflicted CEO of the company in the Northwest (and for his somewhat wary leadership team members), including a masterclass in the assessment process supplied the taste of self-management reality they needed, in order to decide what would be best for their organization. It allowed them to say, "Okay; now we know that self-management will work for us as long as we can shape it to our own culture. We don't have to adopt a particular model. We can land somewhere three-quarters or seven-eighths of the way down the continuum, keep just a small quantum of command authority for certain circumstances, and make self-management our own."

Not every company leader moves full-throttle into self-management with the kinds of progressive philosophies embraced by Fresh Fill partners Rocha and Windecker. Moreover, some companies opt to run self-management experiments only in certain business units, or in pilot programs. Others opt for company-wide initiatives, but in the form of incremental rollouts. These are not halfway measures; they are wise approaches for most company leaders. Having said that, by means of a thorough self-assessment process, *all* company leaders can examine both the business values and the personal beliefs they can bring to the self-management table, in order to determine where on the continuum, at least initially, the company will launch an initiative.

Decision rights will play a large part in that determination. A decision right is the negotiated right to make a given decision, and organizations deal with thousands of decisions. Who makes which decisions, and why? Which decisions require consultation, and which can be made unilaterally? The person best equipped to make a particular decision usually owns the right to make that decision (and should). Without good reasons, managers should not retain decision rights that could easily be transferred or negotiated to an individual closer to the action. This is called "giving up power"—a crucial success factor in organizational self-management.

When managers unnecessarily retain decision rights, it is costly and wasteful—hence, the "management tax" exercise (see box, Chapter 2) that can genuinely help leaders to determine the company's location on the continuum of organizational structure. Unnecessary vertical permission steps for decision-making constitute a huge indirect cost of management and a huge tax on performance. It is possible to limit the scope of a decision right based on who makes the decision or when, where, why, and how that particular decision is made (e.g., based on tradition, risk, or other factors), thereby subtly shifting an organization's position on the self-management continuum. In a radically self-managed environment of agency and autonomy, however, colleagues freely negotiate the allocation of business responsibilities, *including* decision rights.

One of the core responsibilities of a leader, according to philosopher Peter Koestenbaum, is to manage polarities. A key polarity to manage is the balance between massive and incremental change. There is risk in moving too fast, and there is danger in incrementalism. It is crucially important to avoid creating chaos. It's not necessarily smart to just blow things up and replace an existing system with a radically different system. But, if one wants to make progress, it is important to undertake experiments and pilot projects that are more visible than tiny incremental steps. On one hand, there is the risk of chaos. On the other hand, there is a risk of not being taken seriously. There is as much risk in moving too slowly as in moving too fast. Wisdom, experience, and consultation are the leader's friends in these matters.

Assessing What the Workplace of the Future Will Demand

Before you self-assess for organizational change, think carefully about what competencies the workplace of the future will require of its leaders and its self-managing workforce. After all, as companies flatten their hierarchies and the taxonomy of "futurework" expands, it seems clear that organizational effectiveness will necessarily depend, as always, on the choices of individuals. Individual effectiveness will ultimately dictate organizational results whether the governance system of choice is holacracy, teleocracy, sociocracy, workplace democracy, ROWE (Results-Only Work Environment), agile management, horizontal management, self-management, wiki management, radical management, lattice management, or any other approach.

16 NOT-SO-OBVIOUS (BUT ESSENTIAL) COMPETENCIES FOR THE WORKPLACE OF THE FUTURE

1. Initiative

2. Tolerance for Ambiguity

3. Consciousness

4. Contribution Mindset

5. Low Power-Distance Sensitivity

6. Natural Leadership

7. Connectivity

8. Noncognitive Skills

9. Network Nurturing

10. Continuous Learning

11. Leveraging the Power of Weak Ties

12. Internal Locus of Control

13. Polarity Management

14. Humility

15. Curiosity

16. Emotional Self-Mastery

The workplace of the future will demand many individual competencies (effective communication, for example), but there are other crucial, and often-less-visible competencies that will impact one's ability to navigate and perform well in a highly autonomous environment. Before you assess for your own workplace environment, consider these sixteen items:

1. **Initiative.** It's virtually impossible to deliver constructive feedback to colleagues, or effect positive change in process or strategy, without a willingness to take initiative. Taking initiative includes the ability to speak up when necessary. Self-managing leaders have an affirmative obligation to speak up as needed—for example, when observing situations incongruent with the mission, vision, or values of the enterprise. Being a good listener is not enough; the need for initiative also applies to taking action. Alexander Hamilton wrote about the need for "energy in the executive" as a requirement for good government; that same logic applies to highly autonomous individuals in organizations.

2. **Tolerance for Ambiguity.** In a bureaucratic organization, there is a certain amount of security in having people tell you what to do, even if it squelches initiative and, at times, crushes the soul. For some, there can be a certain level of comfort in having ambiguity kept to a minimum. In self-management, however, there is ambiguity around every corner, because no one is directing anyone else. Each worker has a portfolio of stewardships, so to speak, and although there are clear guidelines regarding how to execute *processes*, the freedom and autonomy to improve them abound. That can be exhilarating, but it can also create ambiguity. Having to "feel your way" through situations that are not explicitly clear—called *stigmergy*—is the order of each day. Individuals must sense and respond to stimuli in the work environment. So, workers in a self-managed enterprise not only need to tolerate ambiguity, but those best suited also *embrace* ambiguity and see it as a challenge. Organizational autonomy can be messy as col-

leagues meet new people and learn new ways of working. Negotiating peer agreements that clearly communicate one's purpose, values, and activities takes time and effort. Individuals must make wise choices when seeking commitments from others, and in determining the timing and scope of requests (responders may not give poorly conceived requests a second chance). Similarly, individuals must be careful when agreeing to requests for commitments. Autonomous self-managers need to maintain the right to decline a request without fear of pressure. *It must be okay to say no!* The truth is, autonomy is never as easy as dumping a complaint on the boss's desk and outsourcing the solution.

3. **Consciousness.** It takes real effort to summon the energy needed to pursue one's purpose at work consistently, every day. That kind of energy is akin to the dynamism that entrepreneurs call up to create entirely new enterprises out of ephemeral ideas. It is mindful consciousness that gives rise to awareness and presence. And it is mindful consciousness that is the source of confidence in one's ability to get things done—even in the face of adversity. That means resilience and the ability to focus, to be present in the moment, and to execute with clarity and effectiveness. At its best, mindful consciousness is what performers and leaders of all kinds describe as being "in the zone"—a near-perfect state of focused awareness.

4. **Contribution Mindset.** Generosity of spirit and a desire to contribute are the personality characteristics best suited to a self-managed enterprise. Taken together, they are often

referred to as a "contribution mind-set." Individuals with this mind-set are aware of needs and look for opportunities. They genuinely want to make the world a better place. People with such qualities want to contribute value to their fellow colleagues, offering, "I can help you with that," or, "I can give you some good resources." Peter Drucker talked about a contribution mind-set in his superb little book, *The Effective Executive: The Definitive Guide to Getting the Right Things Done.*[58] A half-century later, that mind-set applies to everyone who wants to be an effective self-manager in a highly autonomous enterprise. W.L. Gore and Morning Star, for example, expect individuals to share relevant information with colleagues as a matter of principle, even when the information has not been requested.

5.   **Low Power-Distance Sensitivity.** "Power-distance" refers to the act of deferring to individuals presumed to have more power than oneself. In a self-managed environment, there is an unofficial hierarchy of credibility which springs from experience, trust, communication, and other factors. That is not the same thing as a hierarchy of power based on command authority. Effective self-managers will find ways to express themselves to anyone in the organization and will listen to anyone and everyone who wishes to speak with them. To avoid communication with a colleague based on presumed status is to cut off the lifeblood of an organization: the flow of information.

6.   **Natural Leadership.** In a highly autonomous environment, relationships, as well as many activities, are purely

---

58   Peter Drucker, *The Effective Executive: The Definitive Guide to Getting the Right Things Done* (New York: HarperCollins, 1967).

voluntary. And in purely self-managed companies, no one has the authority to direct the activities of others. Leadership is exercised through communication, respect, influence, persuasion, and trust. Natural leadership is earned over time and is not an artifact of position or title. So, what is the evidence of true, natural leadership? The presence of followers.

7. **Connectivity.** Effective communication will be always-on/always-near. Autonomous leaders and followers will receive and respond to communication requests whenever possible (it's appropriate to negotiate boundaries around availability). The presence of always-on/always-near communication is a leading indicator of a robust self-organizing network in action. Ken Thompson, author of *Bioteams*, describes this competency as driving a sense of collective ownership coupled with an effective 24/7 "early warning system" for teams.[59]

8. **Noncognitive Skills.** Organizational leaders of the future can learn important lessons from children. In Paul Tough's book, *How Children Succeed: Grit, Curiosity and the Hidden Power of Character,*[60] the author persuasively describes the absolute power of noncognitive skills. Describing what matters most in a child's development, he refers to evidence of the importance of noncognitive, character-related skills, which include grit and curiosity. Because there will always be off-days, resilience matters. In her book, *Grit: The Power of Passion and Perseverance,*[61] psychologist Angela

---

59   Ken Thompson, *Bioteams* (Tampa: Meghan Kiffer Press, 2008).

60   Paul Tough's, *How Children Succeed: Grit, Curiosity and the Hidden Power of Character* (Boston: Houghton Mifflin Harcourt, 2012).

61   Angela Duckworth, *Grit: The Power of Passion and Perseverance* (New York: Scribner, 2016).

Duckworth identified grit as the single most important characteristic of success, more important, even, than intelligence. Grit is essential in the self-managed enterprise, for it teams with curiosity and trying to figure out the best way to do things.

Grit is essential in the self-managed enterprise, for it teams with curiosity and trying to figure out the best way to do things.

9. **Network Nurturing.** In the parlance of Ken Everett, author of *Designing the Networked Organization*,[62] the organization of the future will naturally be a network of networks. Every autonomous leader will nurture and engage with a primary immersive network, nested within or connected to a larger network of networks. Resources and information will flow freely, according to demand. Autonomous leaders will operate with agility and fluidity throughout the entire network of networks because—to put it simply—they will have no other way to get things done. At its core, a self-managed organization is a giant network. The people across the enterprise must nurture the relationships that feed the network, so that they can keep the entire system warm and alive. They rely on the network to get things done, and thus they grasp the importance of helping to feed the thing that feeds them—a never-ending virtuous circle.

10. **Continuous Learning.** With his book, *The Fifth Discipline*, Peter Senge pioneered the notion of highly autonomous leaders nurturing the practices of learning organi-

---

62   Ken Everett, *Designing the Networked Organization* (New York: Business Expert Press, 2011).

zations for strategic benefit.[63] In the twenty-first-century workplace, everyone should be free to develop core competencies in strategy, financial literacy, process management, leadership, teamwork, communication, hiring, negotiation, or any other management discipline.

11. **Leveraging the Power of Weak Ties.** In the enterprise of the future, not everyone will be lucky enough to work in a Dunbar-limited[64] workplace of 150 colleagues or fewer. Even in those workplaces, not everyone will be a friend. Many relationships, in fact, may be transitory. But the leaders of the future will need to know the people with whom they work well enough to successfully broadcast clear, well-received, low-energy messages that keep initiatives on track without resorting to undue pressure or coercion.

12. **Internal Locus of Control.** Psychologists often refer to an individual's internal or external locus of control. A person with an internal locus of control takes personal responsibility for his or her own circumstances. An individual with an external locus of control believes that his or her life is buffeted by external forces and blames fate (or other people) for failures large and small. A preponderance of blaming behavior is a serious performance obstacle. Effective self-managers will have an internal locus of control—they will self-examine how to improve. They will hold themselves accountable.

---

63   Peter Senge, *The Fifth Discipline* (New York: Doubleday, 1990).
64   In the 1990s, British anthropologist Robin Dunbar posited that humans can comfortably maintain only 150 stable relationships at a time.

13. **Polarity Management.** Individual self-managers need to be able to spot and manage tensions and dilemmas in the workplace, of which there are many: detail vs. big picture, tactics vs. strategy, innovation vs. execution, subjective vs. objective, freedom vs. accountability, thinking vs. feeling, and many more. Effectively balancing polarities with dexterity is essential for long-term success.

14. **Humility.** Large egos hinder effective self-management (remember the effect that power has on the brain). A healthy self-respect is essential for confident interaction, and people with healthy self-respect can be humble. Humility is all about the ability to manage one's own ego for the sake of the greater good. It is directly related to having a "We" orientation versus a "Me" focus. Self-managed organizations flourish when people exercise self-control and egos don't run amok. Humility smooths the way.

15. **Curiosity.** This is an essential element of continuous improvement. Every workplace needs its skeptics—the people who are always asking "Why?"

16. **Emotional Self-Mastery.** Milton Pedraza, CEO of the Luxury Institute in New York City, says that this competency, consisting of deep empathy, trustworthiness, and generosity, will allow people to thrive in the workplaces of the twenty-first century.[65]

If this inventory of requisites is anywhere close to being on target, then the job of visionary future leaders in a hyperconnected

---

65   Milton Pedraza, "The Future of Work Manifesto: Self-Management and Emotional Self-Mastery Are The Most Powerful Skills for Business Success in the Next Decade" LinkedIn, June 14, 2018, www.linkedin.com/pulse/future-work-manifesto-self-management-emotional-most-powerful-milton/.

world will be to embed the fundamentals of effective, autonomous self-management into every people process: recruitment, selection, hiring, orientation, onboarding, curriculum design, coaching, performance management, succession planning, career transition, conflict management, leadership development, compensation, and all the rest. Much work lies ahead, but it starts with clearheaded self-assessment of the current workplace.

The No-Limits Self-Assessment Quiz

HOW OPEN IS YOUR CULTURE TO EXPERIMENTING WITH SELF-MANAGEMENT?

Rating Scale:

1. Strongly Disagree

2. Mostly Disagree

3. Somewhat Disagree

4. Somewhat Agree

5. Mostly Agree

6. Strongly Agree

Rate each of the following statements according to the scale above, with one as "Strongly Disagree" and six as "Strongly Agree." Be as honest with yourself as possible. To ensure unbiased results, you might also consider asking your leadership team members or a random sampling of group leaders to take the assessment anonymously. Tally your score (or take the average of all group-member scores for each question) after all responses are complete. To interpret results, see the key on the last page of this chapter.

1: Initiative

1. This organization rewards those who take initiative.

2. People feel free to innovate and improve here.

3. People who take initiative do not feel as though they are "sticking their neck out."

4. This environment encourages people to improve processes and systems.

5. Failure is acceptable as long as people learn from their mistakes.

2: Effort/Perseverance

1. The ability to keep going despite adversity is honored here.

2. People here do not quit easily.

3. People feel good here when they see a project or idea through to completion.

4. Consistent effort is more valuable here than long hours.

5. Making progress, despite obstacles, is one of this organization's success factors.

3: Effectiveness

1. People here pursue their respective missions, whether working alone or with others.

2. People here effectively consolidate discretionary time to enhance productivity.

3. People make the best use of their time by focusing on what they do well.

4. People here choose their priorities well, aligning them with the organizational mission.

5. People here are generally enthusiastic.

4: Continuous Learning

1. People here care about the future of the organization.

2. People here like to renew and refresh their knowledge, skills, and abilities.

3. People here proactively seek and share information.

4. People here enjoy teaching and mentoring their colleagues.

5. People here are up to date in their area(s) of specialization.

5: Creativity/Innovation

1. Most of the work here allows people to be creative.

2. People here feel encouraged to find better ways to do things.

3. People here are not pressured to do things "the way they've always been done."

4. This organization provides resources to appropriately pursue innovations.

5. People here are expected to try new approaches.

6: Collaboration

1. People here check with one another before undertaking actions that affect others.

2. Communications about work issues flow easily and naturally between people here.

3. People here are cooperative and helpful with each other.

4. Information is shared routinely between colleagues, whether requested or not.

5. People here are rarely surprised by new business strategies, people, or processes.

7: Accountability

1. People here hold each other accountable for the standards of the organization.

2. It is rare that people get away with violating the expectations of their colleagues.

3. People do not become defensive or retaliate when being held accountable.

4. Expectations and standards are reasonably clear and defined.

5. It is expected that each person is willing to hold his or her colleagues accountable.

8: Self-Organization

1. Leadership often rotates to whoever possesses the most expertise pertaining to an issue.

2.   People often self-organize into temporary groups to solve problems, improve processes, or pursue strategies.

3.   Work groups here often don't have identifiable leaders.

4.   Work groups often seem to form spontaneously in response to a need.

5.   Work groups here fluidly and dynamically form and dissipate as needed.

9: Adaptability

1.   People here easily adapt to changes of direction.

2.   People here are not invested in outmoded processes, relationships, or strategies.

3.   People here are generally not stubborn or inflexible.

4.   People here appreciate complex challenges.

5.   People here respond appropriately to pertinent new information.

10: Freedom

1.   People here are free to negotiate changes in their work terms and conditions.

2.   People here are free to acquire resources needed to do their work.

3.   The scope of individual decision authority here is reasonable and appropriate for each individual.

4. People here feel they have control over their own work.

5. People here feel they have some input into choosing with whom they will work.

11: Influence

1. Relationships here are characterized by people seeking to understand the other's point of view.

2. Most of the people here are able to express their viewpoints clearly.

3. People usually take the time to explain their requests in a respectful manner.

4. Generally, people here take a long-term perspective with colleagues rather than short-term expediency.

5. The work environment is characterized by good manners and courtesy.

12: Leadership

1. People here work to equip and enable their colleagues to improve.

2. People here make the time and take the effort to earn the respect of others.

3. People here set good examples for others.

4. People here seek to identify, communicate, and implement best practices.

5. People here effectively communicate their vision for new or improved processes or projects.

13: Feedback

1. People here know where they stand regarding their performance.

2. People here know what measures and metrics pertain to their mission.

3. People here are willing to discuss individual and team performance issues with each other.

4. People here iteratively try to improve their performance based on objective measures.

5. Information regarding performance is readily available and accurate.

14: Awareness

1. People tend to ignore artificial boundaries like "departments" in order to get things done.

2. People are aware of other colleagues' activities that may overlap or impact them.

3. New hires tend to get up-to-speed quickly.

4. People in this organization do not usually duplicate their efforts.

5. This organization does a good job capturing and sharing relevant process knowledge.

15: Coaching and Mentoring

1. The people in this organization mentor new hires to help them adjust quickly.

2. Many perceptual differences and conflicts are effectively addressed with appropriate coaching or mentoring.

3. People here accept workplace coaching and mentoring for many purposes.

4. Coaching and mentoring helps people here leverage their strengths and find meaning at work.

5. Individuals here feel that they can reach out to others for wisdom and guidance.

KEY TO RESULTS:

75–300: **Stop and analyze carefully.** Before initiating anything, understand which part or parts of the organization will be amenable to self-management pilot projects or experiments, which parts will not, and why. Always invite, include, and involve people in designing and implementing initiatives.

300–375: **Exercise caution.** Your culture isn't perfect, but it should be healthy enough to thoughtfully enlist amenable colleagues in identifying pilot projects and experiments in organizational self-management. Invite and include them in determining first steps, then involve them in implementation and measurement of results.

375–450: **Full speed ahead.** Your healthy culture should support highly visible self-management change initiatives, so long as leaders involve people affected in creation, implementation, and measurement of results.

CHAPTER 7

ESTABLISHING YOUR SELF-MANAGEMENT PHILOSOPHY AND PRINCIPLES

*If you want to succeed in business, don't get
an MBA. Study philosophy instead.*

—MATTHEW STEWART, FORMER MANAGEMENT
CONSULTANT OF THE MITCHELL MADISON GROUP

WE'VE SPOKEN PREVIOUSLY about the strength of a self-managed organization, where every individual is part of a human network of accountability, responsible to everyone else in the enterprise and to the enterprise itself. But what forms the basis of that network are the *tenets* of the company: the principles and philosophies (core values such as mutual accountability) that serve to undergird the human network.

Sustaining a Resilient Human Network

I like to think of a self-managed network as a spider's web. It may look like a fragile network of threads, yet the spider's web is one of the strongest, most durable wonders of nature. Because of the tensile strength of spider silk, the web of strands is extremely resilient and enduring. Similarly, in the case of self-management, it is the principles and philosophies (the solid "silk") of the organization that undergird the network (or "web") of the workforce, creating an enterprise that is so sustainable that it can support greater and greater performance. *It is an enterprise where there are virtually no limits to the levels of success that can be achieved.* What's more, as the web of networks becomes more tightly spun (company workers transparently interact with ever-greater numbers of their colleagues), the gaps between the strands become narrower and the web becomes denser. That means that there are fewer places throughout the organization where corruption, exploitation, and other workplace ills can creep in.

In a self-managed environment, there could be hundreds of eyes—as opposed to a few designated managers—to catch potential warning signs of trouble.

In a self-managed environment, there could be *hundreds* of eyes—as opposed to a few designated managers—to catch potential warning signs of trouble. Importantly, all the facets of daily operation are carefully spelled out, most often in a constitution-like document or statement of universally applicable business principles within the organization. In that way, the principles and philosophies that underlie the organization's core values are available to all and encourage clarity.

Best Practices and Commonalities

Let's take a look at the core values of various self-managed organizations to see which principles and philosophies were of greatest importance to them, and where the commonalities lie among the values of any number of self-managed enterprises.

W.L. GORE

Consistently ranking in the top tier of *Fortune* magazine's "100 Best Companies to Work For" is W.L. Gore. The innovative manufacturer of high-performance outdoor apparel and related products has relied on a "lattice" organization (basically, a horizontal network of self-managing peers) since 1958. The late Bill Gore established the company's four key principles—clear, simple, and straightforward values—which have underpinned the company's success ever since and are viewable at gore.com. They are:

- **Freedom**. We encourage each other to grow in knowledge, skill, scope of responsibility, and range of activities. We believe that Associates will exceed expectations when given the freedom to do so.

- **Fairness**. Everyone at Gore sincerely tries to be fair with each other, our suppliers, our customers, and anyone else with whom we do business.

- **Commitment**. We are not assigned tasks; rather, we each make our own commitments and keep them.

- **Waterline**. Everyone at Gore consults with other knowledgeable Associates before taking actions that might be "below the waterline," causing serious damage to the enterprise.

HAIER

The world's largest home appliance manufacturer, often termed one of the most innovative corporations on earth, Haier's 70,000 largely self-managed employees run operations all around the globe. According to the Haier website,[66] the company's phoenix-like success—rising from the ashes of a notoriously dysfunctional and unprofitable organization—rests on three of its core values, discussed in greater depth on the site, and crystallized below:

- **Rights and Wrongs**. Users are always right, while we need to constantly improve ourselves.

- **Development Concept**. The twin spirits of entrepreneurship and innovation are at the heart of Haier culture.

- **Interests Concept ZZJYT**. ZZJYT is shorthand for *zi zhu jing ying ti*, a win–win mode of individual-goal combination. We base it upon independent operating units or self-managed teams.

I attended Haier's first International Rendanheyi Model Forum in China in 2017, which modeled the now-successful entities called microenterprises that Haier is creating in domains as diverse as cattle ranching, health care, and video gaming. Key for the company is unleashing innovation throughout the enterprise while avoiding the pitfalls of bureaucracy. Haier strives to create a company brimming with entrepreneurs.

---

66   "Core Value of Haier," Haier, accessed January 17, 2019, www.haier.net/en/about_haier/culture/.

ZAPPOS

Despite its challenges with holacracy, the online shoe and apparel distributor, now owned by Amazon has continually refined its principles and philosophies. Stated on Zappos' website is: *As we grow as a company, it has become more and more important to explicitly define the core values from which we develop our culture, our brand, and our business strategies. These are the ten core values that we live by:*

- Deliver WOW through service.

- Embrace and drive change.

- Create fun and a little weirdness.

- Be adventurous, creative, and open-minded.

- Pursue growth and learning.

- Build open and honest relationships with communication.

- Build a positive team and family spirit.

- Do more with less.

- Be passionate and determined.

- Be humble.

As Zapponian Derek Noel told *Fortune* in 2016, "My worst day at Zappos is better than my best day anywhere else. I can't imagine going back to traditional hierarchy anymore."[67]

MEETUP

Launched in 2002 and recently acquired by New York's WeWork, the Meetup social networking website provides software that allows

---

67   Jennifer Reingold, "How a Radical Shift Left Zappos Reeling," *Fortune*, March 4, 2016, http://fortune.com/zappos-tony-hsieh-holacracy/.

its members to schedule events via a common platform. Core values have undergone several refinements in recent years. Meetup's ABC-styled core values statement is now more detailed and lengthier than those of many self-managed organizations, yet it is certainly unique. According to the Meetup website: *Codifying the values became an ambitious project in itself. But on the other side of it, we ended up with a strong point of view about how we work together and what characteristics matter most when we hire new Meetuppers:*

A—*Always Go for Maximum Impact on Lives*

- **Possibility > Stability**

  We like stability, but we like the possibility of impacting more lives even more.

- **Scale > Edge**

  We like to care for everyone, but we like scaling and simplicity even more.

- **Lives > Money**

  We like money, but we like making money in ways that strengthen the network even more.

B—*Be Brave and Bold*

- **Focus > Spread**

  We like to take on a lot, but we like doing fewer, high priority things well even more.

- **Action > Precision**

  We like precise measurement, but we like acting when measurability is not possible even more.

- **Pushy Loved Ones > Polite Peacekeepers**

  We like not annoying people, but we like confidently encouraging people out of their comfort zones even more.

C—Change the Company

- **Courage > Comfort**

  We like our routines and ways, but we like always improving even more.

- **Risk and Evolve > Protect the Past**

  We like what we've got, but we like making the Meetup of tomorrow even more.

- **Systemic Fix > One-Off Fix**

  We like fixing things, but we like systemic fixes (small and big) even more.

D—Debate and Decide

- **Speak Up > Harmony**

  We like harmony, but we like the better ideas that come from people speaking up even more.

- **Action > Consensus**

  We like consensus, but we like action even more.

- **Commit > Kvetch**

  We like defending our opinions, but we like being open and recognizing when it's time to commit (or switch teams) even more.

E—Empower Everyone

- **Unleash Potential > Control People**

  We like having power, but we like distributing power even more.

- **Owning > Working**

  We like people who show up, but we like people who step up even more.

- **Decentralized > Centralized**

  We each like caring about everything, but we like clear roles and responsibilities even more.

F—Futurize

- **Build Faster Tomorrow > Build Fast Today**

  We like launching, but we like investing to launch faster in the future even more.

- **Growing Roots Together > Live Fast, Die Young**

  We like hard work, but we like working hard sustainably even more.

- **Reputation > Winning by Any Means**

  We like winning, but we like integrity even more.

- **Vision-Led >Fast-Follow**

  We like fitting in today, but we like inventing the future even more.

M—Meetup!

- **Together > Alone**

  We like heroic individuals, but we like rabid, amazing, caring teams even more.

- **Experiencing > Theorizing**

  We like talking about community and Meetups, but we like living it even more.

- **Faces > Screens**

  We like avoiding awkwardness, but the best things happen when people meetup.

MORNING STAR

From its original and basic underlying tenets of (1) Freedom to work happily (noncoercion) and (2) Commitment to colleagues and personal/company mission, The Morning Star Company has refined and further detailed its values in the company's constitution-like document, designed to impart clarity to the entire workforce. In its Colleague Principles on the Morning Star website, the company lists the following seven core values. Please visit the website for review of details not included in the abbreviated version below:

In order to encourage, achieve, and maintain an atmosphere of high integrity, trust, competence, and harmony among all colleagues, customers, and suppliers, each Morning Star Colleague commits to the following:

1. **Mission.** Our Mission is to produce tomato products, which consistently achieve the product and service expectations of our customers in a cost-effective, environmentally responsible manner.

2. **Individual Goals and Teamwork.** We hereby agree to commit ourselves to the pursuit of perfection with regard to our integrity, competence, and individual responsibility. In recognition of each Colleague's personal goal of achieving happiness, each of us commits to pursue teamwork because *Together Everyone Accomplishes More.*

3. **Personal Responsibility and Initiative.** We agree to take full responsibility for our actions as well as those of fellow Colleagues and our overall Mission.

4. **Tolerance.** It is understood that individuals differ in many ways—their values, tastes, moods, and methods to achieve goals. It is agreed that these types of differences between individual Colleagues, which do not directly affect our Mission, will be respected and tolerated.

5. **Direct Communication and Gaining Agreement.** Differences between human beings are a natural and necessary aspect of life, especially in the pursuit of excellence. To gain agreement and move forward, we agree to utilize [a self-managed dispute resolution] process. [See website for comprehensive process details.]

6. **Caring and Sharing.** To the degree Colleagues care about themselves, their friends, and relatives, fellow Colleagues, suppliers, customers, the environment, the Mission, Principles and facilities, etc., each of us will come closer to achieving our personal goals. In caring for others, each colleague commits to (1) share relevant information with others, (2) take initiative to forward information that they believe may be helpful to another's activities, even if it is not asked for, and (3) respond to respectful inquiries made

of them by other Colleagues in a respectful and responsive manner.

7. **Doing What is Right.** Live, speak, and endeavor to find the truth.

Self-Management Principles Are Everywhere, Always

The previous examples of company principles and philosophies reveal certain similarities: They express a desire and intention to provide value for the world at large. And they stipulate the importance of working together in a noncoercive fashion that promotes the opportunity for joy and innovation in one's work, plus responsibility to working colleagues and the enterprise as a whole. While each company's values may differ according to product or service mission, all statements embrace certain principles that are fundamental to life, exist everywhere, and are always operational. (Recall the example about the fundamental principle of gravity: one may choose to deny the existence of gravity and soar off a building roof, but the desire to deny gravity doesn't make gravitational force any less present.) Similarly, companies around the world may choose to align their goals with always-operational principles, such as the human pursuit of happiness and fulfillment, or they may not. But *not* aligning with a life-affirming principle does not make it nonexistent. Thus, self-managed enterprises may seem unique in a largely bureaucratic business world that persistently (and unsuccessfully, I must add) suppresses basic life principles.

Here's a useful thought experiment: Imagine a world where people everywhere have aligned their behavior with humanitarian principles. What kind of world would that be? If everyone in the world abandoned the use of force against other human beings, for instance, we wouldn't need military or police forces, or locks on our

Imagine a world where people everywhere have aligned their behavior with humanitarian principles. What kind of world would that be?

doors. In short, it would be an amazing world. Of course, we know universal adoption of such principles is not realistic—but that's not the point. The point is that *to the degree* people align themselves with civilizing, harmonious, and productive human principles, individuals and their cultures (organizationally and otherwise) are better off. Principles matter.

Self-Management Principles Are Derived from Law

Many of the principals embraced by self-managed organizations are also derived from those that form the foundation of law in cultures where the use of force (coercion) is not tolerated. In most cultures, for instance, murder, kidnapping, theft, and assault are criminal acts. Many acts of duress warrant legal action, as well. Yet, in so many bureaucratic workplaces, duress feels like an everyday state of affairs. Not so in self-managed work environments, where any kind of coercive constraint would only serve to harm workers and, thus, by extension, the enterprise as a whole.

Contract law, too, underlies many tenets of self-managed businesses. After all, the basis of contract law is the contract itself: an agreement to keep one's promise or commitment to another party. Imagine a world where commitments are routinely made—and broken just as quickly: commitments would have no meaning whatsoever and chaos would ensue. In Western culture, great effort and much expenditure is focused on ensuring that individuals and entities keep their commitments to one another, so that the business of daily life does not spin out of control. Imagine again a world where we need little or no policing to ensure that commitments are met: insurance premiums and litigation costs would plummet and productivity would *soar*.

In the workplace, the use of coercion (even subtle forms of coercion) and the absence of commitment-keeping or accountability translates directly to employee anxiety and, ultimately, employee disengagement. On the flip side, the *absence* of coercion accompanied by *confidence* in universal accountability engenders happiness and the freedom to be passionate about one's work. It also breeds innovation in the workplace, thus contributing to the greater good of the enterprise, and creating value for humanity as a whole.

Optimizing on Core Values

With basic life-affirming and law-based principles and philosophies in place, companies are free to optimize on the core values that will set them apart from their competition and make their business goals worth pursuing.

W.L. Gore, for instance, optimizes on innovation. With innovation top of mind, Bill Gore's first-stated core value of freedom was a logical choice. Not only is freedom an ever-present life principle for human beings and a basic tenet of our US Constitution and legal system, but it is also the ground from which innovation sprouts. Hence, the company's statement about the importance of innovation within its Core Value No. 1: "We believe that Associates will exceed expectations when given the freedom to do so." Remember that, true to its principles, W.L. Gore encouraged one of its workers to pursue development of a guitar string product based on a Gore performance material. Another Gore associate created a high-tech dental floss from Gore fiber that now forms the basis of a highly successful product line.

Zappos, a distributor as opposed to a manufacturer, optimizes on customer service. Because of the company's ability to focus on the competitive edge of service, customers can rely on near-flawless deliveries and returns, and the company reaps the benefits in reputation, customer loyalty, and profits.

Polarities in Core Values

Interestingly, within so many of the principles often included in self-management core value statements, there are also polarities or the push-pull of opposing needs. And there is the mandate to manage those polarities.

For example, W.L. Gore thrives on innovation coming from any individual within the company. Yet, acknowledging that with innovation comes a certain level of risk, the company also adopted as a core value a "waterline" principle: "Everyone at Gore consults with other knowledgeable Associates before taking actions that might be 'below the waterline,' causing serious damage to the enterprise." One can well imagine that an individual worker, experimenting with materials and machinery, might unwittingly set off a series of events potentially harmful to the company. But in a self-managed workplace, where a web-like human network of coworkers takes shared responsibility seriously, unforeseen "waterline" disasters are much less likely to happen. That network itself provides the checks and balances commonly absent in more bureaucratic organizations where power trumps shared accountability.

And in a self-managed enterprise such as Morning Star, polarity management is the backdrop for "playing the game of work" which helps the company predict, manage, and strategize around market and world forces that may impact the business for better or worse. In this way, not only are "waterline" issues averted, but competitive advantages are preemptively seized when the push–pull of indicators emerge.

Core Values and the Company Constitution

While virtually all self-managed companies have an expressed set of principles and philosophies that they hold up as their guiding North Star, not all formulate a company constitution around those tenets— but they should. The more mature or established the enterprise, the more likely it is to have seen along the way the need for a clear-cut, fixed document that spells out the details of the company values as they apply to the ins and outs of daily operations. The constitution is, in fact, the bedrock of the company; always there to help support any issues that may come up, while at the same time dispelling ambiguity. Morning Star, for instance, cleanly and precisely spells out the company processes for dispute resolution and dismissal requests. These are processes that may be undertaken by any individual within the company. And because there is no HR department (to impersonally handle such issues), clarity of purpose and process is essential. Anyone at any time may need to refer to the constitution for such process information or other guidance.

Then again, there undoubtedly have been company constitutions that were unnecessarily ambitious to the point of reading like legal briefs. Yet, at its best, the constitution should detail Who We Are, What We Believe, and How We Function. But watch out: if the document becomes one designed to protect company leadership at the expense of the company workforce, it becomes an authorization that essentially negates the entire purpose of self-management—and the human beings who work for the company will know it.

Identifying Your Principles and Creating Your Constitution

The process may sound simple, but serious thought, time, and discussion will help you to form your guiding principles and then construct your company constitution from those building blocks. The general order of things is:

- Start with principles and resist the temptation of many to immediately seek out practices, tools, and systems. Principles are your friend. They will sustain you in tough times, long after practices and tools become obsolete. Principles never change. Principles always work and never take a day off. Trying to implement a self-management initiative without firm principles in place is like building a house without a foundation—it may collapse under the first heavy winds of a storm. Self-management principles start with the concept of free will: that human beings freely make choices in all situations. You'll definitely want a North Star of foundational principles to guide the people in your organization in making those choices.

- Check out the principles of other self-managed (or similar) organizations. You may find enlightenment in any industry or vertical, so look at everything you can.

- Find the meaning of your organization and form your company principles after serious soul searching (What are your own lifelong values and philosophies? What will be your company's deepest purpose?). Discuss your thoughts with your startup, leadership, or retooling team. Consult with everyone you wish, consider all possibilities, and then harpoon the fish—the core values that will be your company's beacons.

- Look at other company constitutions, to get a sense of how companies have applied their principles to their everyday operations and issues.

- Work with stakeholders to develop your own company constitution. Refine it up front and over time, as new issues and considerations arise.

- Post both the company core values (principles and philosophies) and the constitution online and within the company walls where people have easy access. Most self-managed companies proudly post their company values for *all* website and company visitors to see. Some companies embed and call out the company's core values within the constitution, for a single declaration or document.

Back in 1990, when Chris Rufer convened our little Morning Star Company startup team, it was clear to us all that he had been thinking about his life and business principles for years. We had already broken ground on the new factory when he called us together and handed out a three-page document with easy-to-read large type that incorporated his two key principles of noncoercion and commitment. The document also contained some governance language that surrounded those principles. There was a process for resolving conflict, a commitment to be transparent and share information, and a few other important thoughts about good teamwork, striving for perfection, being tolerant, and sharing and caring. (Remember his question to us: What does work have to do with love?) Basically, his handout was all about the two key principles that he deeply believed would engender happiness and passionate productivity in the workplace. He asked us if we had anything better to propose for organizational governance (we didn't). Then we discussed the document, adopted it, and became a self-managed organization on the spot. The language has been refined a bit since but, essentially, it hasn't changed since 1990.

Bill Gore and his wife, Genevieve, started their company sixty years ago in a garage in much the same fashion, and their tenets were simple, too. Both Bill Gore and Chris Rufer believed that the individuals within their companies were walking, talking freedoms. They designed their companies (and their lives) to not only respect that truth, but also to wholly support it. That belief led to the realization that companies don't need to motivate, manage, and "develop" free people who have opportunities and resources always available to them and who manage themselves perfectly well everywhere else. Self-management is all about freedom. The business philosopher Peter Koestenbaum said it best:

> We live in organizations that are more interested in controlling and predicting behavior than understanding it. We view freedom as a problem to be managed rather than the essence of all motivation and creativity. If we can deepen our understanding of what it means to be a human being, we can become leaders who discover great

meaning no matter where we work and no matter what we do for a living.[68]

Crystallize and Finalize the Company Statement

Now that core values of the enterprise have been discovered, and a framework for the company constitution has been erected, it will be easier to tackle the multitude of decisions that come with the first stages of self-management. We've previously discussed the importance of determining where on the continuum of self-management your company (or new self-management organizational structure, if you are retooling) should launch. The following bulleted considerations will help you to crystallize that locus and finalize your new company statements.

CONTINUUM

Command authority and leadership:

- Will your company retain any hierarchy, bosses, or managers?

- Will there be command authority at any level?

- What about unilateral hiring and firing?

- Will people retain formal titles, or will everyone be addressed similarly, from the top down?

---

68   Peter Koestenbaum, *Freedom and Accountability at Work: Applying Philosophic Insight to the Real World* (San Francisco, Jossey-Bass, 2001), xiii. For more on self-examination and leading a self-managed organization with courage, ethics, reality, and vision, see the Leadership Diamond on Koestenbaum's Philosophy in Business website, pib.net.

- Will any leadership responsibility be designated, or will leadership develop organically as people team for projects and tasks, and the individuals closest to the action with the most appropriate skills emerge as natural leaders?

These questions will require you to carefully consider the continuum that runs from absolute command authority on the left (slavery, which is not an option) and zero command authority on the right (total self-management wherein you rely on trust, respect, influence, and persuasion). Understand that, because command authority is binary—you either have it or you don't—where you opt to retain it in your self-managed organization, you will need to set very clearly communicated boundaries around which kinds of commands can be issued, and who can issue them.

CULTURE

- Do you believe everyone is a manager in his or her own life, bringing those same skills right into the workplace? (Or do you believe that some people still need to be "managed"?)

- Will your company culture foster respect for all humans with no demographic distinctions such as "white collar" or "blue collar," etc.? (In other words, can good ideas and improvements come from anywhere at any time?)

- Will colleague commitment, responsibility, and initiative be critical to your enterprise?

  - Do you believe it will *enable* self-management and build the kind of culture you envision?

  - Will people be seen as professionals; stewards of the enterprise; business owners of their areas and co-owners of the enterprise mission as a whole, regardless of legal ownership structure?

- What about information sharing? Will your company culture encourage hoarding and hiding, or will information sharing be obligatory or by request?

- Will the company's self-management processes be open to analysis, experimentation, and improvement by all?

- Have you seriously considered the importance of language in your self-managed environment and in your company documents?

  □ Language goes hand-in-hand with company culture: Will you be able to foster the human spirit of innovation while still calling your people "employees" (people who work for pay), or will terminology such as "colleague" and "associate" resonate more deeply?

  □ Will the language in your company documents and interactions inspire and uplift, or will you unwittingly perpetuate some levels of repression?

- How important is freedom? Do you believe that people are "walking freedoms" who manage their lives and families, day in and day out? (In other words, do you believe that people do their best work when they are free to do it well and are not coerced?)

- What about fun? Clearly, fun is a top priority at Zappos, for it ranks number three on the company's list of its ten core values. Ask your initial self-management team to take a vote; fun comes up in the top five priorities more often than not.

- What are your thoughts on collaboration, hard work, and enlightened competition or *competère* ("learning together") across colleagues and departments or divisions? *Competère* is especially key to the formation of your company's culture, for it means that your stakeholders (including your customers) learn together and educate each other all along the way. As for enlightened competition, it does not mean you give your customers the lowest price they can get; it means that you negotiate vigorously and educate your customers well about the realities of the marketplace. You strive to give them the best *value* in that marketplace.

- When disputes arise, how will they be handled? More conventionally, by managing and policing, or via a self-managed resolution process that can escalate if needed?

- Will your process be key to your company values and culture?

ENABLING SELF-MANAGEMENT EFFECTIVENESS

- Will commitment, responsibility, and integrity underlie all stakeholder interactions in your company?

  - Will it be essential that people stand by their word and their agreement to deliver (integrity)?

  - Will colleagues put their long-term commitments to each other in writing?

- Will communicating effectively, sharing information, and taking initiative be both colleague-to-colleague and colleague-to-enterprise responsibilities that excite and engage people? Will they feel a sense of belonging and psychological safety?

- Should commitments be requested or on-demand? That is, should commitments be sought only through influence and persuasion? Communication philosopher Fernando Flores argues for a "conversation-for-action" communication model of speech acts, which involve making an offer or request which another is free to accept or decline—a radical notion in many command-and-control organizations. If accepted, a commitment is made to fulfill the promise—and commitments are bold acts of intention with a structure and lifecycle.[69]

- Will the personal/commercial values of each member of the workforce need to align with the company's mission, values, and vision? Or will the company operate successfully with those who do not necessarily support the company's mission, values, and vision? If so, how will that work?

- Will human emotion be squelched in the workplace? Leaders of self-managed organizations want people to be passionate about their work—and passion means emotion. Simply put, happiness underlies the success of self-management. As does control: people being in control of their *own* lives and work. And neuroscientists now know that people cannot make decisions without emotion—so think twice before you hearken back to treating human beings as

---

69   Harriet Rubin, "The Power of Words," *Fast Company*, December 31, 1998, www.fastcompany.com/36313/power-words.

automatons. High emotional intelligence is also a characteristic of most successful self-managers.

- Will the company develop and distribute/post colleague principles, a constitution, or similar?

- Will performance measurement or a real-time reporting mechanism be accessible to all so that there is real-time feedback for course correction, information sharing, and transparency?

- Will a new-colleague selection process (hiring) be handled largely by those who will work most closely with the new colleague?

  □ Will all those who will work with the new hire have a voice in the process?

- Will there be mentoring, training, and new colleague orientation and onboarding?

- Will the company offer opportunities for colleagues to develop their strengths?

  □ Opportunities for desired future career configurations?

  □ Opportunities to develop greater social and emotional intelligence?

- Will social technology play an important role in enabling self-management in your enterprise?

  □ Will you employ meeting alternatives such as OpenSpace and the World Café to unlock innovation and leadership?

DECISION RIGHTS

- Will the company leader or owner retain some strategic decision authority, or will colleagues negotiate the ownership of decision rights, including strategy decisions?

- Who will handle proprietary information?

  - Will that access be restricted? If so, by what means?

- Who will have responsibility for business process improvement and management?

COLLABORATION

- What will be the importance of commitment to the company's customers across colleagues?

- What percentage of the organization's "surface area" will touch customers and external resources?

- What role will collaboration play, and to what extent?

- How, precisely, will the self-management environment help individuals to collaborate?

Embracing Your Company's Reason for Being

Examining the aforementioned issues, one by one, will not only help you to clarify your self-management goals and processes for the first stages of your initiative, but the process will also intensify your focus on your combined personal and business purposes—your enterprise's raison d'être. But before you jump to the enterprise's reason for being, it's important to think about your *own* purpose and meaning.

Work, for the average person, says Koestenbaum, is external to life and is, therefore, experienced as a constraint on life itself. In his landmark work, *Leadership: The Inner Side Of Greatness,*[70] Koestenbaum explains that time pressure is actually the pressure of existential guilt: people feel stress because they are not living up to their meanings—and bureaucracy thrives on guilt. When you find your meaning, instead of managing time from the outside in (as myriad books and articles prescribe), you *are* time—an inside-out approach. Time slows down, enabling you to be focused in the moment, addressing challenges and opportunities with speed and intention and allowing you to integrate multiple facets of your life at an unprecedented level. This may sound esoteric, but it's surprisingly basic, as in *basic to who you are*. Koestenbaum's philosophical approach to business has inspired "ah-ha" moments for many a business leader; *Leadership: The Inner Side of Greatness* is recommended reading for any company head or owner pondering personal purpose and meaning.

Next up: the implications of self-management—or anticipating what may happen, post roll-out.

---

70 Peter Koestenbaum, *Leadership: The Inner Side of Greatness* (San Francisco: Jossey-Bass, 2002).

CHAPTER 8

SELF-MANAGEMENT IMPLICATIONS (OR, WHAT TO EXPECT)

*Greater than scene is situation. Greater than situation is
implication. Greater than all of these is a single, entire
human being, who will never be confined in any frame.*

**—EUDORA WELTY, NOVELIST, PLAYWRIGHT,
AND SHORT STORY AUTHOR**

FOR OUR PURPOSES, one of the cleanest definitions of the
amorphous term "implication" is the one I located on Vocabulary.
com: "an implication is something that is suggested, or happens,
indirectly. Usually used in the plural, implications are effects or consequences that may happen in the future."

I couldn't help but pin the Eudora Welty quote, above, to this
chapter. Welty may have been thinking about playwriting when she
crystallized the importance of implications. But implications speak
to self-management, too. We can rework Welty's quote to read:
"Greater than the environment in which one works is an individual's

situation—how he or she works. Greater than situation is implication—what happens indirectly, because of that work. Greater than all of these is the single, entire human being who will never be confined in any frame—including an org chart!"

There could be any number of implications when you launch a company in self-managed mode or re-tool an organization toward self-management; the wide-ranging list of cultural aspects I've asked clients to consider is usually thought-provoking.[71] But let's look at some of the most common implications you will encounter, and want to consider, up front.

Challenges to Effective Self-Management

When Fresh Fill's Brian Rocha kicked off the hiring process for his California convenience store launch, he understood some of his hires would not work out. Rocha navigated the initial hiring process holding firm to his company's philosophies and principles. Yet, he realized not everyone would be a "best fit." He knew he would likely have to let some people go, and probably early on.

Every company has its issues with personal characteristics that are not well-suited to the company culture. In a work enviornment where self-management is the context for company culture, there are additional aspects to consider.

THE POWER-SEEKER OR POLITICIAN

The first one that comes to mind is an individual who enjoys power. This character trait is a bad fit for self-management simply because in a fully self-managed enterprise, everyone's voice is equal to everyone

---

71   Check it out in an infographic format at www.alivewithideas.com/blog/
       infographic-twenty-eight-components-to-effective-organisational-culture.

else's. Weeding out the power mongers can be especially challenging when a company transitions from command-and-control to self-management. The weeding is crucial, however, if you are to create an enterprise that thrives on change and innovation. As renowned business thinker Gary Hamel has observed, the prerequisite for change is that people must be willing to give up power—and many (most) managers don't willingly give up power. The power-ingrained personality type is often more prevalent in middle management than in top leadership, if only because middle managers often have risen up the org chart, enjoying mounting doses of power (remember those addictive shots of dopamine?). What's more, the *fear* of losing control only exacerbates the situation for a power player in the leveled playing field of self-management.

Power-seekers and politicians aren't well-suited to a self-managed enterprise, either, because there's no place to hide. When you voluntarily negotiate and agree on purpose, job content, roles and responsibilities, scope of decision-making authority, and how performance will be transparently measured, your coworkers will expect you to live up to that contract. If you're spending a lot of time on political maneuvering and thus are not fulfilling your contract, it's going to be painfully obvious to everyone, and *someone* is going to call you out.

Power-seekers and politicians aren't well-suited to a self-managed enterprise, either, because there's no place to hide.

THE FEARFUL OR CHANGE-AVERSE INDIVIDUAL

Clearly, moving to self-management can be a problem for those accustomed to having some manager hand down decisions about their work hours, schedule, terms of employment, etc. They will suddenly be expected to participate in those decisions and shoulder more responsibility, and they may experience anxiety about that. The whole point of self-management is that *everyone* is a manager which, for each working colleague, creates an additional layer of account-ability plus more thinking, work, and opportunity for initiative. Those who enjoy challenge thrive; those who do not, often don't.

Having said that, there are also individuals who are niche-oriented: those who have been left to work on their own for years, focusing on a particular area of subject matter expertise (R&D, for instance). Niche-oriented people may be somewhat change-averse, yet can still be very valuable in a self-managed environment, where roles are sculpted by agreement. Their agreements can even specify preferred modes of social interaction (along with job content and company contribution), as long as the agreement is voluntarily agreed upon by the individual and his or her working group.

THE PASSIVE AND PASSIVE-AGGRESSIVE COLLEAGUE

People who are passive personality types or generally lack initiative may find self-management challenging mostly because self-man-agement relies heavily on constant communication. Constant com-munication requires initiative on the part of transmitters, seekers, and receivers of actionable information. If you lack initiative, then you may not be a proactive communicator, essential to effective self-management.

Passive-aggressive individuals give lip service to the idea of self-man-agement in general, but then don't deliver to colleagues. "I'll try to get back to you on that" sends up red flags immediately. To a working colleague, it means, "I don't care about you. You don't really count in my book, so I may just let you *think* that I respect your request while I ignore you." These people may be procrastinators or individuals with hidden agendas; either way, they operate passive-aggressively, undermining effective self-management.

SMOOTH DELEGATORS OR PSEUDO SUBJECT MATTER EXPERTS

One of the hiring challenges some clients face is bringing on people who have subject matter expertise *and* experience. Such individuals may be mid-career, and generally come from traditional (often Fortune 500) organizations. Therein lies the rub: they frequently have been delegators who tell other people what to do, and have learned to be smooth talkers along the way. When the boss leverage is removed, these hires can flounder because they don't know how to deliver direct value to their colleagues. A supply chain expert, for instance, may not be able to deliver supply chain skills at all; he may only be able tell others what to do, while schmoozing his superiors.

People vary tremendously in their motivations, mind-sets, and approaches to life. A self-managed environment of agency, autonomy, accountability, and freedom should be beneficial to virtually anyone. Some will leverage that freedom to the hilt, others not so much. Fortunately, self-managed enterprises don't have to be perfect. They just have to be better than traditionally managed organizations, where 67 percent of the workforce is disengaged and the management tax is wasting $3 trillion per year in lost productivity.

Three Superpowers of Effective Self-Management

EVERYONE A LEADER

Self-management does indeed require leadership; it is an essential element of an effective, self-managed organization. In a self-managed organization, leadership can come from anywhere at any time. Leadership is not determined, it emerges dynamically (as needed), just as it does in life outside of the workplace. A friend, Dr. Lori Kane, describes being on a hot team at Microsoft, interfacing with multiple business units on their most-pressing issues. On any given day, the members of her team would describe feeling the pull of leadership, but could not necessarily identify which team member was leading.

Self-management does indeed require leadership; it is an essential element of an effective, self-managed organization. In a self-managed organization, leadership can come from anywhere at any time. Leadership is not determined, it emerges dynamically (as needed).

The essential point here is that leadership muscle in a self-managed organization is constantly exercised, while in organizational hierarchies, leadership muscles atrophy as people get lazy and mistake the power of ordering people around (not a unique skill) for true ability to steer, guide, and spearhead a given task or project.

In a self-managed ecosystem, leadership can spring forward from any place at any time. One enterprising Morning Star technician, for instance, recently theorized a better way to handle chemicals. He designed a system, created a proposal, solicited support and funding, and implemented a project that paid for itself almost immediately.

That kind of natural leadership is what gives self-managed organizations such a compelling strategic/competitive advantage.

In a self-managed enterprise, everyone is free to lead and anyone can be a leader—the true measure of leadership being whether or not one has followers. Leadership often revolves around subject matter expertise, but not necessarily; it may revolve around a required competency such as emotional intelligence. At Morning Star, colleagues are responsible for *any* issues that penetrate their scope of awareness (called a "ring of responsibility"). Opportunities for innovation, continuous improvement, relationship-building, resource acquisition, process execution, regulatory compliance, and all the other domains of business require a degree of leadership. In a self-managed ecosystem, leadership emerges when and where it's needed, often serendipitously and from unexpected sources. That's the power of self-management.

COLLECTIVE WISDOM

It is important to point out that because self-management taps the collective intelligence of an entire group, it aspires to include many kinds of personalities: introverts and extroverts alike, for example. Daniel Pink, in his work *Drive: The Surprising Truth About What Motivates Us,*[72] maintained that *every* personality type should benefit from greater autonomy, freedom, and purpose, along with the opportunity to achieve mastery. The self-managed enterprise can, for instance, benefit from the expertise of even the most timid soul, if that person can bring value to the whole and fashion an agreement that is acceptable to all. After all, in every enterprise, *someone* has to

---

72   Daniel Pink, *Drive: The Surprising Truth About What Motivates* Us (New York: Riverhead, 2009).

drive in the rivets. In a self-managed enterprise, every last riveter can seize opportunities for improvement all along the way.

Collective wisdom must be shared. People who are ideal hires for a self-managed organization are also those who are willing to "speak truth to power." Even in a self-managed enterprise, some employees will be perceived by their peers as larger, more charismatic, or more confident than others; it's only human nature. Yet, what levels out the perception of natural leaders is every worker's willingness to speak up and speak out to anyone in the enterprise, for the good of the enterprise. Not only does each member of the workforce have a right to speak up; in self-management, everyone has an *obligation* to do so. Bill Gore saw this obligation as key to W.L. Gore's core values when he stipulated the waterline principle—the obligation of all W.L Gore colleagues to "watch the waterline" and speak up when they observed something that could potentially sink the company ship.

It's not enough to be a good listener; as Peter Drucker noted in his book, *The Effective Executive: The Definitive Guide to Getting the Right Things Done*, one must be willing and able to speak up and insist on being heard and understood, to be effective.[73] It's also wise to implement voice-activating mechanisms such as ombudsmen, and social technologies like Open Space, that make it possible for everyone (including introverts) to be heard.

MAKING AND KEEPING COMMITMENTS

Fernando Flores, the Chilean-born linguistics and computer researcher is regarded as the godfather of commitment-keeping. His research and experience taught him that commitments are speech acts that consist of making someone an offer, which that individual

---

73   Peter Drucker, *The Effective Executive: The Definitive Guide to Getting the Right Things Done* (New York: HarperBusiness, 2017), xxiii.

is free to accept or decline. If the offer is accepted, a commitment to fulfill a promise has been made. Flores collates these speech acts into sequential elements that comprise the structure of commitment conversations to build trust, integrity, and ultimately performance.[74]

Flores has variously referred to his theories as "commitment-based management," "conversations for action," or "ontological design" combining philosophy, neuroscience, and linguistics.[75]

Virtually every leader regards integrity as a crucial stakeholder and employee characteristic. What is the source of integrity and trust? Keeping commitments. Stephen Covey's book *The Seven Habits of Highly Effective People: Powerful Lessons in Personal Change* describes integrity as "making our actions conform to our words" (related to but distinct from honesty, which is about making our words conform to reality).[76] Integrity means making sure that one's actions reflect what they have already communicated they will do for others. Reality matches words. People who keep commitments consistently brand themselves as reliable, and develop reputations as persons of integrity.

Keeping commitments creates real economic value and makes individuals and the enterprises within which they work more valuable. The value of a commitment depends on the level of trust one has in the fulfillment of the commitment.

The value of a commitment depends on the level of trust one has in the fulfillment of the commitment.

To put it in human terms, assume there are two otherwise identical production managers, each making $100,000 per year, but

---

74   Lawrence M. Fisher, "Fernando Flores Wants to Make You an Offer," *Strategy+Business*, November 24, 2009, www.strategy-business.com/article/09406?gko=ce081.
75   Ibid.
76   Stephen Covey, *The Seven Habits of Highly Effective People: Powerful Lessons in Personal Change* (New York: Simon & Shuster, 2013).

Manager A is 100 percent reliable in keeping commitments, and Manager B is only 80 percent reliable. Manager A ensures that sales always receives the agreed-upon product mix for customers. Manager B commits to supply sales with the correct product, which would have resulted in a $25,000 profit but, on one of his unreliable days, produces faulty product instead, which sells at a $35,000 loss. The enterprise would be completely justified adjusting salaries and paying Manager B less than 80 percent of Manager A's salary (at any salary level). That 20 percent unreliability has already cost the company significantly more than $20,000—in this example, $60,000 for one missed commitment. The takeaway here? Unreliability is profoundly costly. Reliability is extraordinarily valuable.

The fact is, the cost of doing business with integrity-and-reliability-branded people is lower, and thus transacting business with such individuals is more profitable. On the flip side, the more profitable it is to do business with someone, the more people will want to work with such individuals, and the more opportunities those individuals will have. That's how value increases, both commercially and personally. It's also how individuals and companies grow.

Commitment-making and commitment-keeping are critical self-management skills and there is bona fide history and research around the concept of commitment-keeping. Commitments are affirmative speech acts. Commitments have structure. Commitments have a lifecycle. Commitments are one of the most misunderstood and dysfunctional concepts in the life of most organizations. Think about it: a major problem in many (if not most) organizations is that people can be sloppy about the way they make and fulfill commitments, resulting in suboptimal levels of trust, excessive frustration, and major disappointment. Trust flows from proven integrity, which flows from effective commitment-keeping and communication.

At Morning Star, commitment-keeping is one of the two core principles of self-management, making it at least half the foundation of enterprise governance. It is a mission-critical business success factor. *That's* why commitments are important.

Recruiting, Screening, and Selecting New Hires

Bringing on new people is a self-management implication that confuses many, but it shouldn't. The goal here is not to trash every last vestige of conventional command-and-control, but to find and bring on talent in a way that delivers great results. In self-management, this involves a process wherein those closest to the work have the ultimate responsibility for choosing their optimal working colleague. (Who better to assess an electrician candidate than fellow electricians?) Still, that doesn't mean there aren't numerous ways to go about the hiring practice, especially when a company is in launch mode.

Looking again at the Fresh Fill startup, for instance, Brian Rocha was explicit when he said something to the effect of, "I'm not going to give up all command-and-control right away. I'm going to get this thing up-and-running first. After things are running well and the kinks are smoothed out, I'm going to hand the reins over to everyone else." That is precisely what he did, although he bounced plenty of ideas off others first. But Rocha saw those initial hiring steps as the job of the founder. After that, his job became part of the network, like anyone else's.

Firing in a Self-Managed Organization

Firing, or termination, is a self-management implication that perplexes many until they realize that a truly self-managed process eliminates common complications and repercussions of termination that occur in a more conventional workplace. It is more humane (though certainly more involved) than announcing "You're fired!"

In pure self-management, firing is a departure request process that honors and respects the dignity and voice of every individual in the organization. No one is subject to the whim of a superior; no one can be unilaterally, arbitrarily, or capriciously terminated by another. The fear of unjustified termination is gone, replaced by a very serious protocol of due process.

That process relies on request-and-response—initially, one-to-one (direct) request-and-response. It also involves a good deal of ambiguity: To terminate a coworker, someone has to have the courage to make the initial request to a fellow colleague, *without knowing how things will turn out*. Let's say I notice that the company's security guard has left his station and has caused the premises to be unguarded, voiding the company's insurance policy. The action is unacceptable. Therefore, I, as his colleague, may ask him to culminate his services to the enterprise (the request). He may agree or disagree (the response). Either way, the ambiguity of the situation can be challenging, for I have no idea how the security guard will react. The request is also confidential, although at Morning Star, for instance, I may consult with a confidential advisor (known as an ombudsman), a colleague designated for this purpose, among others.

If the guard admits he was negligent and agrees to go, we may negotiate the terms of his departure; two weeks for us to find a replacement, for example. But let's say the guard refuses my request and disagrees with me. We then move on to a mediator, a fellow colleague we both agree on and trust to help resolve the differing viewpoints. (Everything in the process is negotiable.)

Importantly, there is no status in this process: the initiator can be a riveter, while the responder can be the organization's financial controller. The process can be challenging. Requests can be bold, but when information or evidence is clear, the process can work effectively and justly because it is a direct offshoot of a self-managed organization's core tenets to respect the individual rights and dignity of all. In essence, the process removes HR (and thus depersonalization) from the equation and allows people to negotiate for themselves.

The outcome is never assured, but the important thing is to keep the process human. At Morning Star, we once called the process Resolution of Conflicts; we now call it Gaining Agreement, which is more about what humans strive to achieve as they live or work with others. Of course, no "process" applies if someone is brandishing a weapon, is intoxicated, or is threatening assault and battery; common sense dictates an immediate call to 911. Society and the legal system impose that responsibility on us.

Embracing Ubiquitous Innovation

Self-managed organizations prize people who are willing to innovate and improve wherever they see an opportunity. Innovation—so vital to a competitive twenty-first-century enterprise—springs from initiative and imagination. Technology will generate limitless opportunities for individuals to create value in the twenty-first century via virtual reality, realistic virtuality, augmented reality, and myriad other paths that rearrange time, space, and matter in endlessly imaginative ways. (Read about this in Kim Korn's *Infinite Possibility*, referenced in Chapter 2.)

In conventional companies, most people know precisely where any advances will come from, largely because only specific departments and individuals are tasked with the honor of moving the company forward through innovation. But in a self-managed organization, the innovation genie is released: new product and service ideas, and new pathways around obstacles can come from anyone, anywhere, at any time. For generations, employees in traditional bureaucracies have bemoaned the fact that they cannot express the depth and breadth of their abilities as they clock in, clock out, and toe only the lines they have been allotted. In self-management, with every individual (not merely a select few) encouraged to help move the company into the future, the potential for competitive edge is statistically vast.

Take the Chinese appliance giant, Haier, for instance. From a failing refrigerator manufacturer, the CEO (visionary business strategist Zhang Ruimin) eliminated 10,000 middle manager positions and created a giant innovation platform of over 4,000 self-managed teams (called microenterprises, or MEs), many of which use direct customer feedback to spin out new ideas the way one of the company's pulsating washers spins water. His goal? To make Haier the most competitive company of its kind in the world.

Many of the Haier teams are multidisciplinary, market-facing units that work incessantly to meet the needs of a rapidly changing customer base, served by support (node) microenterprises which facilitate that focus. With customer feedback pouring into the MEs from internet-enabled appliances all over the world, Haier teams are free to innovate. Some MEs have become incubators for new products and services. Haier MEs have moved into video games (Thunderobot), hospitals, cattle ranching, and more. Ruimin's vision of innovation that knows no bounds has become Haier's *raison d'etre*.

Because the company sees innovation as key to its success, it unlocks the imaginations of its people across the entire enterprise.

The results are impressive: Haier is now the number-one appliance brand in the world, a veritable No-Limits Enterprise.

Relinquishing Conventional Decision-Making

Sooner or later, the question of who makes the decisions and who has a voice in a self-managed company crops up. And it should, because self-management requires the relinquishing of command-and-control decision rights, and the return of those decisions to the individuals closest to the tasks at hand—those carrying out the work of the enterprise. Everyone gets his or her brain back.

The issue of decision rights is an implication that must be considered early on. If you think back to my story about the company that was immersed in the self-management retooling process when the CEO suddenly knuckled under to middle-management pressure to drop the entire initiative, you can see where the decision rights rubber often meets the road: squarely at middle management. That's because middle management is the stratum where people tell others what to do, and middle managers may be loath to give up their power.

Still, the issue of decision rights is not one for only those bureaucratically entrenched organizations seeking to retool as self-managed enterprises. Decision rights are a serious consideration for startup companies, too. Think about Fresh Fill, for instance, where company founder Brian Rocha determined that he would retain decision rights during the initial hiring process and then relinquish them directly afterward to ensure a purely self-managed business model. Or, consider that W.L. Gore's Bill Gore oversaw a largely self-managed organization while retaining specific decision rights for the company leaders, as does Haier's Zhang Ruimin.

Today, the disruption by millennials in the global workplace—a generation of young people who seek meaning and purpose at work—demonstrates that even in an entrenched vertical such as the financial sector, employees may never again bend to outright command-and-control. The internet has reinforced this disruption by making information readily available to all; what you don't want employees to know can no longer be filtered through a single bureaucracy or hierarchical structure. Virtual teaming, new modes of self-organizing, disintermediation beyond Uber and Airbnb, plus new technologies coming down the pike (blockchain, Bitcoin, artificial intelligence) will only make command-and-control more obsolete, as all of these things, and more, align with self-management like puzzle pieces snapping into place.

Yes, the collaborative and consultative decision-making process of self-management may be more involved than were the simple "just do it!" commands handed down in organizational bureaucracies. Yet collaborative decisions tend to be *better* decisions, as journalist James Surowiecki argues in his bestselling

> *Collaborative decisions tend to be **better** decisions.*

book, *The Wisdom of Crowds: Why the Many Are Smarter Than the Few and How Collective Wisdom Shapes Business, Economies, Societies and Nations.*[77] Importantly, the demise of command-and-control decision rights does not mean that, in self-management, every person has a veto over every decision. It does not mean that people can stall decision-making with foot-dragging. But decision-making *is* a question of ethics and justice in self-management: it means that to the degree possible, you need to involve people and include them in things that

---

77   James Surowiecki, *The Wisdom of Crowds: Why the Many Are Smarter Than the Few and How Collective Wisdom Shapes Business, Economies, Societies and Nations* (New York: Anchor Books, 2004).

are going to affect their work lives. For the No-Limits Enterprise relying on the best decisions possible, collaborative and consultative decision-making happens to be self-serving, as well. For decisions made by individuals, the question is: Who is the best person to make this decision?

Rings of Responsibility

"Rings of responsibility" refers to a way to visualize the idea that in a self-managed organization, everyone is responsible for everything, to the degree he or she becomes aware of the issues. In this visualization, the primary ring is an individual's domain of work; the things she was hired to do. That's where a worker's concentration and focus is directed, and where colleagues can expect that individual will make her greatest contribution. But if she becomes aware of an issue outside of her primary ring of commitment, then she owns that issue, too, and it's incumbent upon her to deal with it (hence, W.L. Gore's "waterline" stipulation in that company's core value statement). In a self-managed organization, everyone is part of the whole and everyone is responsible to the whole, as well as to their colleagues in their agreed-upon performance arena.

Death to the Performance Review

In the conventional business world, managers have traditionally looked backward in time to review employee performance in an annual review or the like. It's generally been a "sandwich" affair: superiors tell their workers about all the positive things they noted in the preceding months, then they present the list of negatives, shake hands and hope their charges will be motivated to do better. Deflated after such an experience, those reviewed rarely are motivated to improve.

The good news is that performance management is changing radically, even in some conventional firms where the focus is shifting to a forward-looking process, rather than a backward-looking critique. In its quest to enhance work/life balance, Deloitte, for instance (number eleven on *Fortune*'s 2017 "Best Companies to Work For" list), has made the transformation from annual review to timely, rolling performance feedback. And rightly so, for reviews can be weighted, influenced by hidden agendas, and tainted by a whole constellation of corporate ills, such as withholding titles, compensation, and rewards. For all those reasons and more, the annual performance review must die.

In self-management, there's simply no need for a bureaucratic, heavy review process. In any given space of time, colleagues will know precisely who is important to the success of the team's work, and who isn't. Self-management is essentially a self-weeding and self-promoting process wherein those who are passionate about and committed to their work succeed and progress, and those who fall glaringly short don't.

We can learn from Deloitte: the company boiled its performance evaluation process down to four simple items:

1. Given what I know of this person's performance, and if it were my money, I would award this person the highest possible compensation increase and bonus.

2. Given what I know of this person's performance, I would always want him or her on my team.

3. This person is at risk for low performance.

4.   This person is ready for promotion today.[78]

The process is forward-looking because team members ultimately ask themselves, *Would I want this person on my team in the future?* If not, working peers can urge their colleague to step up performance or else find something to do that is a better fit.

Managing Conflicts and Differences

In a conventional organization, workers can complain to a manager or supervisor. But how will they resolve differences in a self-managed workplace? In a self-managed environment, there is no such thing as employee discipline, for that would imply that there is a superior somewhere to dole it out, or the existence of coercion—both of which are nonexistent in a self-managed workplace.

As in so many of the implications we've described, to resolve differences, self-management demands proactive action on *everyone's* part, although there are any number of ways to handle uncomfortable situations rather than just tolerate them. An organization can, for example, offer conflict management training to all of its workers. In self-management, there is a powerful incentive to seize initiative and handle issues directly and fairly. Yet, as Morning Star does, an organization can make use of an ombudsman process wherein colleagues receive confidential advice before they handle issues one-on-one. Colleagues can also take it upon themselves to request that a coworker amp up his conflict management skills to resolve an issue in a timely fashion. If private discussion does not resolve a difference, a mediation process with an agreed-upon third-party mediator can

---

78   Jena McGregor, "What if you could replace performance evaluations with four simple questions?," *The Washington Post*, March 17, 2015, www.washingtonpost.com/news/on-leadership/wp/2015/03/17/deloitte-ditches-performance-rankings-and-instead-will-ask-four-simple-questions/?utm_term=.aa2c72c6a6f0].

be initiated, or a panel of agreed-upon peers can be convened to help decide an issue of contention.

The point is that the process your organization chooses will work as well as your people work to make it effective. Outside of the workplace, individuals grapple with such issues all the time— whether to directly approach someone with an issue, for instance. In the end, the options around conflict management are *value* choices: Do the benefits of pursuing self-managed conflict management action outweigh the challenges of leaving people to behave in ways that are not congruent with effective, ethical self-management?

Dynamic vs. Traditional Budgeting

Self-managed organizations should think beyond traditional, cycle-driven budgeting processes. In self-management, the formal budget-approval process inherent in a conventional organization becomes much more organic and dynamic. Like the living, growing thing that it is, the self-managed enterprise knows when it needs sustenance, and for what. Funds and resources need not be automatically allocated anywhere; corners need not be cut to make the numbers line up; variances need not be subjected to microscopic study. Requirements are assessed only on a need-by-need basis by those most closely associated with them, by the peers affected by the decisions, and by those with a broad scope of commercial understanding and responsibility for strategic and financial processes. Tasks, processes, and initiatives that are imperative require resources; those that are not, may not. Together, colleagues determine what lies in-between, and how those items should be funded.

Self-managers roll up numbers at least monthly, and project years into the future to provide clarity about an organization's financial status at any moment time. The Beyond Budgeting Round Table is leading the charge worldwide to replace traditional budget processes with those such as dynamic, event-based budgeting based on the real-time needs of business. It's not that numbers are unimportant—to the contrary, they are crucially important. It's just that number processes should serve the business, not the other way around.

Work as Fun

My favorite implication of self-management is the one that Chris Rufer first suggested to us, his first team members, when he first introduced us to the idea of self-management: that work should be *fun*. (He told us that he would know people were enjoying their work when he could see the whites of their smiles.) Rufer went on to describe his philosophy of work as a dynamic adventure—a game in which exciting, enterprise-expanding things happen daily, helping colleagues to successfully guide their company into the future.[79] In fact, the notion of work as fun has become so integral to so many of today's self-managed businesses that employees routinely stipulate fun as a core company value when they set about identifying those tenets. Zappos is not alone in listing fun among its top core values. And Morning Star is so well known for its colleagues' love of fun that it has been chronicled in the book *Different Work: Moving from I Should to I Love My Work*, by Lori Kane and Bas de Baar.[80]

---

79   Charles Coonradt, *The Game of Work: How to Enjoy Work as Much as Play* (Layton, UT: Gibbs-Smith, 2012).
80   Lori Kane and Bas de Baar, *Different Work: Moving from I Should to I Love My Work* (Seattle: Amazon Digital Services, 2012).

Self-Management Education
for Sustainability

If you say that in a self-managed work environment everyone is a manager, then the implication is that you're *expecting* people to be able to manage themselves in that commercial environment. But that may not be entirely fair without providing assistance and education in certain areas. One way to amplify the self-management skills people may already possess is to help them develop business savvy, which necessitates business education for individuals. This kind of education also serves to help self-management sustain and perpetuate itself as new hires come on board and people move about the network of teams and functions as needed.

At Morning Star, we created a mini MBA program, consisting of approximately one hundred hours of course work designed to give people skills in the various disciplines of management: planning, organizing, controlling (in the financial sense), selecting, and coordinating. There were modules in strategy for planning, financial literacy for controlling, and business process improvement for coordination. We also created modules in general business skills for teamwork, leadership, communication, negotiation and mediation, and effective interviewing.

We made sure to package the education in a way that would honor self-management and the colleagues' commitment to be effective self-managers in the Morning Star environment. Understanding that our colleagues were already managers in their own lives, we designed the educational experience to *augment* those management skills, to help them be successful self-managers in the commercial work environment, too. It was impressive to watch mechanics, forklift drivers, and salespeople learn the nuts-and-bolts of ROI calculation, debits and credits, negotiation, and effective interviewing. When they learned strategy, it wasn't just about business strategy—it was also about building a strategy for one's entire life, holistically. Any of the mini-MBA graduates would have been equipped with the knowledge needed to start their own successful small business. And they were equipped to use those skills at work. That's the power of a learning organization.

Technology will be a major component of self-management education in the workplace of the future. Tony Bingham, the CEO and president of the Association for Talent Development (ATD, formerly ASTD), says, "The implications [of new technologies] for the talent development profession are enormous. We are uniquely positioned in organizations to identify skill gaps, create plans and programs to address those gaps, and identify what is needed to be competitive. As a profession, we must be diligent in understanding how technology impacts the work happening in our organizations so that we enable and empower the unique value that humans offer in creating cultures that are agile and change-able."[81]

Adaptive learning, the use of artificial intelligence platforms to proactively customize content delivery for individual learners, is one of the hottest topics in development today. Another hot development topic, *microlearning*, is the delivery of contextual support and content in the platform-neutral form people need when they need it to help them do a job (microlearning expert Shannon Tipton defines microlearning as "short specific bursts of right-sized content—trying to target the content toward the problem we are trying to solve").[82]

Non-stop, relevant learning will fuel the sustainable, No-Limits Enterprise of the future.

---

81 Tony Bingham, "The Future of Learning Influences the Future of Work," ADT Tech-Knowledge, October 31, 2018, https://techknowledge.td.org/insights/the-future-of-learning-influences-the-future-of-work?_ga=2.109846853.1343798032.1544659067-2079249097.1543518429.

82 Shannon Tipton, "Interview with 'the Queen of Microlearning' Shannon Tipton," interview by Ger Driesen, aNewSpring, January 4, 2018, https://vimeo.com/249711484.

CHAPTER 9

MAKING THE CASE FOR SELF-MANAGEMENT

Joy does not simply happen to us. We have to choose joy and keep choosing it every day.

—**Henri Nouwen, Dutch Catholic priest, professor, writer, and theologian**

YOU, THE COMPANY LEADER or member of the company's leadership team, have dedicated time and thought to the idea of self-management in your workplace. Maybe you have read what you could get your hands on, attended conferences or webinars, bounced some initial thoughts off others, grappled with the radical notion of abandoning centuries-old command and control, and wondered aloud about millennial disruption in today's business world. Or, in reading *The No-Limits Enterprise*, this may be the first time you have entertained the notion of self-management. No matter: you have long had a deep, abiding sense that the workplace is broken, that too many people spend their lives toiling joylessly to collect a paycheck they will then hand off to mortgagors, car finance companies, and the like. For some time now, you have suspected that your company's ability to soar in the national or global marketplace is tethered by age-old conventions, when it could be set free to achieve almost anything.

You are ready to share what you think and know. You are ready to make the case for self-management.

Making the Case: Who Should Be Involved?

When a company leader begins to ruminate about self-management for his or her organization, there is nothing to dictate who should be brought in, in the early stages of that consideration process. As we've discussed previously, the company owner or leader may have been gathering information about self-management for some time; may have been self-assessing personal and business principles and philosophies; may have been reading helpful material and attending conferences (or may have been sending emissaries to collect such information on his or her behalf). In fact, it is not unusual for the whole idea of self-management to spring first from another individual on the leadership team and be brought to the company head for consideration.

At some point, however, the company leader is going to want to reach out for reactions, feedback, impressions, advice, and arguments from trusted or respected senior colleagues, company stakeholders, personal advisers, and key influencers who will be most helpful in widening the information circle. That said, this kind of communication is an art, not a science, and there are no hard-and-fast concentric-circle guidelines.

In my first book about self-management, *Beyond Empowerment*, "Todd" (my fictional BerryWay CEO protagonist) consulted with a cross-section of advisers that made the most sense to him as he was about to launch his company. In fact, it was one of one of Todd's personal friends who had originally suggested that he set up an advisory board of trusted mentors to advise him on crucial issues in general, and in an informal, helpful way. As he was constructing his processing facility and thinking about what his organizational structure might look like, Todd asked three individuals to act as his informal advisory panel: his primary mentor, the designer of his company's core equipment, and the VP of Operations at a large distributor that was Todd's one long-term customer. All three agreed enthusiastically, happy to be helping someone they liked and respected, as well as pleased at the opportunity to be involved in one of the largest manufacturing startups in the area in more than a decade. These individuals were indispensable during the initial search for key positions in the organization. They also served as sounding boards for Todd's ideas about self-management.

Clearly, for the leader of a startup, an effective advisory panel can be culled from any number of places: the industry at large, the leader's friends and family, experienced and informed acquaintances and mentors, key operations experts, and more. The leader of an existing organization who is considering a transition to self-management may face greater challenges, however, as he or she looks for those who will be most helpful (and least harmful) to an initiative in its seedling stage. In that situation, it is important to look to stakeholders—those who will be impacted by the change—and even more important to cherry-pick the initial team. That's because a company leader serious about a transition to self-management will soon need the message carried out to the people. If those first stakeholders (senior management or not) are not on board, then they can kill the initiative before it ever has a chance to root and sprout. Eventually, stakeholders who are not gung-ho may be encountered, and the goal will be to persuade them to at least experiment with the concept of self-management.

A Consultant Can Help You Make Your Case

An organizational self-management consultant can help with business case-making, organizational assessment, education, and implementation assistance at various junctures in the process. There is no right or wrong time to call in the self-management cavalry.

An organizational self-management consultant can help with business case-making, organizational assessment, education, and implementation assistance at various junctures in the process.

I have been contacted very early on when a company leader has just heard about the concept of self-management through a business acquaintance, at a conference or during a seminar or webinar, or through reading books or perusing the media. Intrigued, he or she will want to know more and may reach out for a phone conference or in-person meeting, one-on-one or with leadership team members in tow. Some leaders and institutions only want a self-management learning session or masterclass. Some require implementation assistance or experiment design. Other companies are seeking periodic phone or online contact, as needed, for troubleshooting.

Certainly, in large businesses seeking to retool a sizable organizational structure (especially where there may be the reconfiguration or elimination of middle-management positions), a great deal of thought and planning is necessary to ease the process. Companies in this position often find the assistance of a consultant invaluable as they make the case to the various levels or rings of stakeholders. The experience a consultant brings to the table—especially with issues such as key influencers or resistance to change, for example—can be invaluable early on and can help to ensure that the initiative is not plagued with problems or stopped dead in its tracks.

Consultants also have tools at their disposal, such as organizational network mappers, that can help to unlock the identities of key people in the organization who may make or break the process. Often, these are proprietary tools, yet even those more accessible tools (OrgMapper, OrgNet, and the Net-Map Toolbox, used by the World Bank to aid development in third-world countries) may require training and expertise that few people possess.

The contextual background a self-management consultant brings to the table, not to mention the know-how to predict roadblocks (and the antennae to sense them), can help any leadership team progress smoothly through its initiative. Even early on, the consultant can help that team to "sell" its self-management case to the workforce in ever-widening circles. Because the universe of management consultants is vast, but the circle of those consultants focused *specifically* on organizational self-management is limited, it is essential to look for specialists, not generalists. If you have no personal recommendations from others who have worked with self-management consultants, then it may be helpful to start your search by scanning social media, reading articles or books written by those focused on self-management, or tracking down webinars, seminars, and conferences at which they speak. A Google search for "self-management in the workplace," for instance, brings up numerous entry points to self-management consulting expertise.

Selling Baby Steps

Yes, there have been organizations that have moved their more-conventionally organized enterprises "whole hog" to new governance structures. Zappos immediately springs to mind, with CEO Tony Hsieh's 2013 pronouncement of the company's earth-shaking shift. Recent media coverage has made it clear that Zappos' enterprise-wide move toward the right side of the continuum has generated some issues for the online retailer. Some of those challenges were doubtless created by the gargantuan size of the shift, with all areas of the enterprise expected to align with the initiative.

The implementation challenge that Zappos has experienced is a primal fear for most company leaders and workforces considering a move to self-management, or even a move to a more networked governance structure. Anyone attempting to internally "sell" the concept of self-management, for instance, will assuredly come up against such fears. Ironic, since it's not necessary to make a "whole hog" shift at all.

If we start with the proposition that no business needs or wants chaos, and that no business should tolerate chaos, a completely legitimate approach is that of moving smaller or well-defined areas of the enterprise to the right of the continuum, one or two chunks at a time. The advantages to this stepping-stone approach are many and include better discernment of pushback and under-the-radar opposition; more time for inclusive, high-quality conversations, better management of the initiative as a whole; and (no small matter) an infinitely smarter way to market successes, one by one, to the rest of the enterprise, before bringing other departments or divisions on board. Stephenie Gloden and her team at the University of Phoenix proved that it's possible to create a new island of effective self-management in an ocean of traditional hierarchy.

Even in the case of a small, wholly innovative startup such as the convenience store Fresh Fill (Los Banos, California), CEO Brian Rocha employed the idea of "baby steps" to ensure the success of his launch. Aware of the fact that so many aspects of his concept store would be untested, he chose to control the initial hiring process in a more conventional manner, opting to release control of that process gradually, after he was assured of creating a solid workforce platform from which to progress. Yes, he could have put a core leadership team in place and immediately handed over the recruiting and hiring functions. But because he knew that each and every hire would be his startup's "face to the customer," he understood that each would be instantly critical to success and might even have to be revised quickly. When it came to staffing his self-managed enterprise launch, some stepping stones were definitely in order.

Most groundbreaking change throughout history has, in fact, been forged via small, considered steps forward. Interestingly, as we are speaking here about moving bureaucratic organizations away from a "slaving away at work" mode and toward freedom of self-determination, collaboration, and full accountability, I can't help but think of the many and disparate steps that were needed to move an entire nation from genuine slavery, to freedom. In fact, abolition first surfaced as far back as the late 1600s as Quakers in Pennsylvania and New Jersey began to congre-

Most groundbreaking change throughout history has, in fact, been forged via small, considered steps forward.

gate to discuss slavery and its incompatibility with the principles of Quakerism. The movement spread throughout the Quaker population over the decades as people read, studied, and discussed the issues. Eventually, the Quakers concluded that slavery was wrong and immoral and needed to be opposed; the idea of abolition then took root and became a battle cry. Yet, it all began with small steps toward changing minds and blazing new trails.

When you set out to make your own case against "slavery" in the workplace and in support of a happier, more impassioned, and productive enterprise for all, keep the concept of stepping stones prominent in the dialogue.

Start Here: 20 Case-Making Points

There are countless benefits to self-management over bureaucracy, as we have seen throughout this book, and they range from the genuinely altruistic (improving and enriching the lives of every stakeholder of your enterprise and making the world a better place for all) to the utterly self-serving (creating an enterprise whose bounds of success are virtually limitless). Some of the points you would doubtlessly want to present when making your case include, but are not limited to:

1. **Bureaucracy (command and control) is out of sync with** the twenty-first-century workplace and is irretrievably broken. Bureaucratic hierarchies will not be able to compete in a world that is changing as rapidly as our world now is. The amount of energy and time required just to keep command and control and bureaucratic administration in place will not be sustainable, going forward. The business world will belong to the most nimble, agile

companies with self-perpetuating and naturally organizing work environments that encourage commitment, collaboration, and innovation from all corners of the enterprise.

2. **Mindless bureaucracy is wasteful of human life.** The hours of an individual's life are the only resource that is completely nonrenewable. Aside from the ethical and moral implications of squandering a life, bureaucracy consumes employee time and energy that could be made available for things that *do* matter—including being passionately productive in pursuit of an enterprise mission and personal happiness.

3. **Human beings are still "slaving away" at work** although slavery has been outlawed in the Western world for over a century. Aside from the waste of human life such oppressive environments demand, and in light of how few millennials will buy in to such environments today, isn't it simply time to end virtual slavery in the workplace? Isn't it time to free the workplace from bureaucracy and better equip it for the future we now face?

4. **The Gallup organization has reported that 67 percent** of workers in the US workplace are disengaged from their organization at any given time, with up to 16 percent of those workers actively undermining the organization through insubordination, gossip, negative social networking, absenteeism, and even sabotage.[83] The hard-dollar cost of the disengagement has been pegged at close to a

---

83 "State of the American Workplace," Gallup, 2017, https://www.gallup.com/workplace/238085/state-american-workplace-report-2017.aspx?g_source=link_NEWSV9&g_medium=TOPIC&g_campaign=item_&g_content=State%2520of%2520the%2520American%2520Workplace.

half a *trillion* dollars in lost production each year.[84] Self-managed organizations do not struggle as much with these disengagement issues because workers negotiate their own personal commercial missions aligned with the mission of the enterprise. Self-managed workers are not compelled to labor; they create their own terms of engagement in their work. It's called the exercise of free will.

5. **Disengagement trickles down to customers.** When companies don't care about workers, workers don't care about the company. Increasingly, employee dissatisfaction is trickling down to the consumer level and impacting customer perception of the company, customer satisfaction, and, ultimately, enterprise competitiveness in the marketplace. With employee disengagement at all-time highs, this poses a very real threat to the viability of an enterprise.

6. **Human beings are not "man hours" or "human resources."** Companies including Amazon and Disney have experienced censure and damaging press coverage from performance metrics that dictate brutal levels of execution speed in the workplace (the legacy of Taylor's scientific management).[85] Via the internet, corporations' employee management practices are now wide open to public opinion and outcry, legal action, and stockholder reaction.

---

84   Ibid.
85   Charlie Parker and Brittany Vonow, "Warehouse of Horrors: Amazon warehouse life 'revealed with timed toilet breaks and workers sleeping on their feet," *The Sun*, November 27, 2017, www.thesun.co.uk/news/5004230/amazon-warehouse-working-conditions/; Steve Lopez, "Steve Lopez: Disneyland workers answer to 'electronic whip'," *Los Angeles Times*, October 19, 2011, http://articles.latimes.com/2011/oct/19/local/la-me-1019-lopez-disney-20111018.

7. **People naturally self-manage in their everyday lives** and are capable of the same kind of self-organizing for the benefit of the enterprise mission and their own personal commercial missions.

8. **When people love what they do,** that love is shared with the customer and the world at large.

9. **Human beings naturally seek to explore and innovate.** To repress or manipulate humans in the workplace is not only wasteful of human life but, paradoxically, is also counterproductive to the mission and goals of the enterprise. When innovation can come from anywhere and everywhere, the enterprise knows no boundaries to success (a true No-Limits Enterprise).

10. **Empowering people is still retaining control of them**; freeing people to responsibly operate under their own power benefits the enterprise as well as the world at large as workers extend those positive behaviors beyond the workplace. This is sometimes called "organizational adulting."

11. **Enterprises have been allocating untold hours and dollars on employee management solutions** that would not be needed without bureaucratic rule in the workplace (such as annual performance reviews). Removing these issues from the workplace frees up the enterprise to become more agile, nimble, and competitive—a No-Limits Enterprise.

12. **Enterprises have been unwittingly paying huge sums of money annually**—an indisputable "management tax"—

for their superfluous layers of managers. When people are free to manage themselves, this money can go directly to the advancement of the enterprise and its stakeholders instead.

13. **Unnecessary layers of management have spawned workplace ills** such as power-mongering and political maneuvering that do not serve the enterprise or the workforce but generate the need for ever more layers of management and control.

14. **Millennials are disrupting conventional employment models** and forcing the most stalwart and bureaucratic verticals, such as investment banking, to scramble for recruitment, hiring, onboarding, and retention solutions. Millennials are largely unwilling to sign on to conventional work environments with limited work/life balance. The reality is that the baby boomer workforce is disappearing and is being replaced by people with entirely different expectations who will not suffer command-and-control. Refusal to accept this reality is tantamount to forcing people who have never seen a rotary phone to rely on one.

15. **As cheap labor becomes scarcer due to immigration reform**, it will become more and more important to be able to attract self-managing talent to the workplace, eliminate superfluous and costly layers of management (the "management tax"), and engage and retain workers. Older cost-cutting measures will prove short sighted.

16. **Following vs. leading in a fast-moving marketplace.** Corporations that used to retain their positions on the *Fortune 500* for decades are now losing ground or falling

off the *500* in a matter of a few years. Other companies and whole industry sectors are facing the end of their viability (Sears, Kmart, JCPenney; the entire large brick-and-mortar retailing sector) or else are facing acquisition. Even the disintermediators Uber, Lyft, and Airbnb may soon be disintermediated by blockchain technology, enabling direct contractual transactions between individuals providing goods and services. Far-sighted companies envisioning the future will lead their packs; short-sighted followers may be the inflexible and obsolete Kodaks of tomorrow.[86]

17. **When the enterprise aims to serve *all* of its stakeholders**, customers are the beneficiaries, for they receive true value at a fair price. Serving customers at the expense of all other stakeholders (e.g., workers) eventually erodes the value of products and services and trains customers to perceive the marketplace unrealistically.

18. **In a self-managed organization, there are no designated bosses because there are bosses *everywhere*.** There is no need for superiors to demand or encourage accountability because everyone is responsible for his or her own personal commercial mission, and thus everyone is responsible to everyone else and to the enterprise itself.

19. **In a self-managed organization, there is no need to design and maintain vertical communication channels**; communication occurs naturally throughout the organically organizing network as needed for collaboration, conveying performance information, sharing market indi-

---

86   For more on the future of work, see "Welcome to a Future Designed for Self-Management: 11 Catalysts" in Chapter 3.

cators and opportunities, and more. A self-managed organization is self-sustaining.

20. **Self-management is not only for small, progressive companies.** All companies—local, global, complex, or mammoth—are comprised of individuals charged with executing their jobs well and being accountable for expected results. Whether it's the internationally lauded W.L. Gore, the rags-to-riches Haier Group, the radically self-organized Brazilian conglomerate Semco Partners, the pioneering nurse-led health care firm Buurtzorg, the online meeting scheduler Meetup, or a new local convenience store model like Fresh Fill, self-management works, and it can work very well. Those who insist that The Morning Star Company, for instance, only "smashes tomatoes" are turning a blind eye to the presence of mathematicians, chemists, and thermal process engineers hard at work in a complex environment under the scrutiny of forty to fifty regulatory agencies. Morning Star, like most large companies, maintains multiple logical business units. They're agile, fluid, and adaptable, not rigidly immutable and bureaucratic. Their purpose is to enhance shared learning, create execution focus, and drive economic thinking, decision-making, and accountability. A larger or more-complex implementation of self-management may take longer and be more detailed, but size and complexity are not inherent barriers to implementing self-management—they are simply challenges to be met.

CHAPTER 10

BRINGING SELF-MANAGEMENT TO LIFE: 12 REAL-WORLD COMPONENTS

I really do believe that working together
works, and it's amazing to me.

—**ALAN MULALLEY, FORMER PRESIDENT AND**
CEO OF THE FORD MOTOR COMPANY

MAYBE YOU SUPPOSED that the simplicity of self-management demands complex steps for implementation, officially endorsed by self-management authorities, or scads of proprietary software to enable a more progressive (flatter) organizational scheme.

On the contrary: holistic self-management does not require rigid and involved implementation steps. It does, however, require a thoughtful, cleanly planned and clearly communicated implementation process, plus vigilant stewardship to prevent slide-back into the many counterproductive hallmarks of bureaucracy.

The fact of the matter is, there are many ways to implement self-management, and we've discussed a number of general approaches—incremental rollouts, for instance.

The important thing is to get the foundational goals of self-management right. That is why this book has been largely focused on the reasons for self-management, what makes it work so well, how it makes a true No-Limits Enterprise possible, and how it can help to change our lives and the world in which we live, one workplace at a time.

12 Components of Implementation

The components of self-management implementation—and we offer twelve of them here—are not, as I have said, hard and fast. They are ideas and suggestions. After reading Chapters 1 through 9, these steps will seem logical, maybe even simplistic, to you, for you have already become well acquainted with the thinking and self-assessment processes behind them. Our discussions throughout have also demonstrated how various company leaders have chosen—for their own excellent reasons—to modify these components. They modify them for the verticals in which their businesses reside, their talent pools, their physical locations in the nation and the world, their product/service offerings and customer base, and for their own company mission and philosophies.

Some company leaders, for example, chose to pull in consultant assistance early for leadership team training. Others opted for consultant help later, for rollout support or solely for periodic consultation. One company owner elected to retain control of the initial workforce hiring process, another chose to hand off that function at the earliest opportunity and then add himself to the ranks of his colleagues.

The essentials here are to keep your eye on the goals and tenets of self-management, and work to construct a rigorous process designed to nurture a thriving, humming, self-perpetuating network of impassioned, engaged human beings (call them peers, colleagues, associates, or whatever works best for your organization). If you've already worked through the foundational processes of your self-management initiative and have sold the concept to the leadership team and the entire organization (including pertinent stakeholders within, and allied with, the organization), then you're ready to experiment.

The overarching themes that make an effectively self-managed organization possible are transparency, accountability, and clarity. The components that follow are intended to instill those themes in the organization and make them real.

> *The overarching themes that make an effectively self-managed organization possible are transparency, accountability, and clarity.*

NO. 1—IDENTIFY THE PLAYERS

Who are the people who need to be involved? Enterprise stakeholders are anyone or any entity impacted by your enterprise, including (but not limited to) company leadership, workforce, affiliates, vendors, customers, facility servicers, stockholders, community members impacted by your business, etc. Which of these individuals or groups will need to know about any organizational change—even an open and experimental initiative? Your planning will need to take those people into account.

And when it comes to rolling out any self-management initiative, clear and systematic identification of those involved in specific tasks and/or processes (your *personal* stakeholders or your working colleagues) is of paramount importance. Those identifications make the effectiveness of a peer agreement, central to coordinated self-management, possible. Who are those individuals who will be the most closely associated with the work that you, as a colleague of the enterprise, are doing? Which individuals are highly likely to be providers of resources and inputs to your processes? Which people will most likely receive the outputs of your processes and work? Self-management presents a whole new way of thinking about and ensuring the success of collaboration, partnering, and teaming. It's about thinking *horizontally* in terms of providing value to customers, not *vertically* in terms of bureaucracy.

NO. 2—INTRODUCE THE CONCEPT OF ORGANIZATIONAL SELF-MANAGEMENT

If organizational leaders envision a self-management initiative but have not yet shared it with people, it will be crucial to engage in ever-widening circles of meetings and deep dialogues, to get the idea of self-management "out there" and exhaustively address questions and concerns about the concept.

"Concept introduction" meeting sizes should not be large—say, about five to twenty-five individuals for each gathering. Careful thought should be given to the structure of the meetings, the information the attendees may have in hand beforehand or may receive during the meetings, and the responses to potential questions. A leader needs to be honest; if you don't know an answer to a question, just admit it and promise to find out.

Remember that directives are counter to the entire concept of self-management, so if you ask a workforce to keep their minds open to the concept of self-management, then *your* mind should be open, too. Change is never easy; give people time to get used to your ideas and proposals. Make your concepts vivid and relatable. Consider alternatives to traditional meetings, using social technologies such as Open Space and World Café (see item No. 9). Invite, include, and inspire. Create a vision of a desirable future state that invites interest and curiosity.

Make sure to give everyone easy and open access to leaders. Welcome concerns, questions about ramifications, suggestions, and ideas. Your goal is to apprise people of the realities: constraints and potential challenges certainly, but especially the unlimited opportunities available as a result of taking a road less traveled. You may want to have a trusted advisor or two on board to give you feedback about your communication strategy and execution.

After the leadership team has blessed the self-management experiment, some see the widening circle of communication as an excellent time to have a consultant on hand who is experienced in self-management opportunities and challenges. The consultant can not only address all possible questions and concerns from the workforce but, in smaller or breakout groups, can also make use of interactive, experiential workshops to help bring self-management theory to life and make it real.

Often, just opening the dialog and eliciting ideas and suggestions proves valuable and helps stakeholders of the enterprise to see the prospect of self-management as an exciting new challenge. At University of Phoenix, for instance, one group leader came up with the idea of launching a book club as a microcosm of self-management. More about this in Item No. 6.

Finally, it's a contradiction in terms to use force to impose a system of organizational self-management, which rejects the application of force. A big part of the problem with traditional command-and-control bureaucracy is that it causes leadership muscles to atrophy. When one has the power to simply impose his or her will on another, it's easy to bypass the hard work of actual leadership. Leaders build strong leadership muscles through dialogue, trust, respect, and communication. Imposing a self-management *diktat* from on high is a contradiction in terms.

NO. 3—DETERMINE SCOPE

The determination of scope can not only be key to the success of a self-management implementation, but pivotal to the buy-in of the self-management concept before it gets to the implementation stage. Unless the self-management initiative is attached to a startup (and even though the appliance giant Haier Group executed a successful, comprehensive rollout across a global workforce of 70,000)[87], my personal advice is to resist the temptation to go "whole hog," especially if your business model involves a significant number of core processes.

Take the time to roll out any initiative or experiment in thoughtful stages. Remember, this is not just to achieve a smooth rollout, but also to make possible the marketing of successes along the way, which can prevent undermining or out-and-out sabotage by naysayers before the initiative can achieve a strong foothold. Naysaying typically crops up around decision rights (No. 7), as individuals loath to give up bureaucratic power become increasingly uncomfortable. So, use smaller incremental steps to give people time to get used to the idea of distributed power and self-management.

Finally, any initiative or experiment must be large and visible enough to have a positive impact, but not so large and cumbersome

---

87   Hu Yong, Hao Yazhou, Des Dearlove, and Stuart Crainer, *Haier Purpose: The Real Story of China's First Global Super-Company* (Great Britain: Infinite Ideas, 2017).

that it creates chaos and confusion. Leaders must proactively manage this polarity sleekly, to preserve gains and avoid unnecessary risks.

NO. 4—IDENTIFY THE WHY

Behind the overarching mission of the enterprise are the missions of the various areas, teams, and affiliates of the enterprise that support the overall company mission. Reinforcing those missions are what we call the separate *personal* missions of all those who work within the enterprise and negotiate their "contracts" with their working colleagues. Each personal mission is essential to the success of the enterprise because it aligns the personal goals of the worker with the goals of that worker's team, group, area, and the enterprise as a whole, creating a self-perpetuating win–win–win scenario.

The perfect alignment of the enterprise's multi-level missions is what makes the self-managed enterprise flexible, nimble, agile, and incredibly strong. The supporting missions are dynamic and fluid, constantly changing and adapting to keep in line with the company mission, precisely the way a vehicle is designed to stay aligned with road, driver, and destination. Think of a racecar, for example: when every element of the car is working at its optimal and most innovative level—engine, suspension, aerodynamics, tires, driver, and each tiny component—the car not only hugs the road, but new records are also achieved.

Going through the exercise of identifying the why can be extraordinarily revealing. I once worked with a small executive team that had been working together for five years. After identifying their respective personal missions, one leader turned to another and said, "I had no idea that's why you're here!" Personal missions must resonate not only with the owner of a mission, but also with those to whom the mission owner relates. Effective, self-managed teamwork demands no less.

NO. 5—IDENTIFY THE WHAT

If identifying multi-level missions is the "Why," then identifying individual process accountabilities is the "What." These account-abilities encompass what you do, and why and perhaps how you do it. It may sound like stating the obvious, but when you think about your time spent in bureaucratic organizations, you'll realize that you had no idea what many of your peers in an organization did there. You may also have been aware of people who were hired for a purpose that was never clear to others, and so their intended job (unhappily) got lost in the shuffle. In self-management, your personal process accountabilities are those outputs for which a colleague agrees to be fully accountable, including performance results. They are variously called KPIs, metrics, measures, or "the numbers." (Google and many other tech companies use a system called OKRs: Objectives and Key Results.) In this section, we'll call them "measures."

The measures should be ongoing and transparent scorecards that gamify performance so that an individual and his colleagues can, at any time, see the score and ensure that the individual is keeping his commitments to his peers. (Morning Star drew inspiration from the book *The Game of Work* by Charles Coonradt.)[88] It should be noted that the measures are not necessarily just *available* for review; peer agreements may detail which individuals are *directly responsible* for their review, and at which intervals. Remember though, all members of the enterprise are always accountable for any concern or issue that enters their scope of awareness. Measures, then, are vital tools for the

---

88   Charles Coonradt, *The Game of Work* (New York: MJF, 2014).

self-managed organization, ensuring that little can slip through the cracks or, as in the case of W.L. Gore, penetrate the hull below the waterline. In our new age of virtuality, augmented reality, and other ways of perceiving the world, measures can also consist of video, audio, and image content to convey performance (for example, video interviews with customers to evaluate satisfaction and happiness).

I always suggest that people identify measures that are meaningful to them, the health of the business, and their peers. All involved need to actively measure whether things are getting better, improving, getting worse, or staying the same. The scorecards that colleagues choose can be anything that works for them; no one dictates how to measure the processes for which they, in fact, are stewards. Measures should simply be as objective as possible. And benchmarks are important.

At Morning Star, for example, the measures are called Steppingstones, because colleagues consider them steppingstones to perfection, Morning Star's ultimate benchmark in all areas. Morning Star colleagues may never achieve absolute perfection, but they reason, "Why would we want to aim for anything less?" A boiler, for instance, will never generate steam at 100 percent efficiency (that boiler has not yet been invented), but 100 percent efficiency is a goal, and the game is to see how close one can get to perfection.[89]

Perfection for an efficiency measure is 100 percent efficiency. Perfection for a cost measure is zero dollars. Gamifying against perfection is a way to liberate blue-sky innovation thinking. An entire organization full of innovators theorizing ways to radically slash costs or boost efficiencies provides a powerful strategic, competitive

---

89   Perfection in golf is to shoot an eighteen, but it seems unlikely that anyone will achieve that score.

advantage. It can also be a lot of fun for people playing the game of work.

NO. 6—CREATE A STRUCTURE FOR COMMITMENT-MAKING AND COMMITMENT-KEEPING

Commitment-keeping is supremely important because it constitutes half the foundation of self-management itself. Self-management is all about the constant flow of requests and commitments back and forth between and among colleagues, which forms most of the substantive conversation about work. Well-constructed commitments include negotiation of conditions of satisfaction, performance, reciprocal declarations of delivery and acceptance, and closure.

Commitments may be long term, recurring, and continuous. These commitments are readily memorialized in a peer agreement. Other commitments may be short term, ad hoc, or singular. These other types of commitments, even if not recorded, are absolutely critical to organizational success. It is imperative that self-managers develop understanding and expertise in the speech acts that form the foundation of effective commitment-making.

IT unit leader Stephenie Gloden of University of Phoenix was searching for an organizational approach to help her team overcome the counterproductive aspects of hierarchy when she came across my book *Beyond Empowerment*. She came up with the idea of forming a book club as a way to get her own leadership team to read the book and see what pieces of self-management they could adopt to transform their environment. Her team reviewed the philosophy and practices of organizational self-management in the book and adopted a transformation project, which took a year to successfully implement as a team. It began with socializing the concepts with peers, while figuring out how to effectively relate to the larger, hierarchical organization. Colleagues developed informal operating-level agreements with each other. These agreements comprised how they wanted to treat each other, how they would depend on each other, and how they would hold each other accountable. Colleagues learned how to step up, and leaders learned how to step back and give people space to solve problems themselves.

When I work with companies to ensure their self-management initiatives will be successful, we spend a good deal of time on the lifecycle and structure of commitments, for they are extremely powerful tools in self-management. The flow of commitments is the lifeblood of every organization. Simply put, *commitments are the way work gets done.*

In a masterclass, we look at various types of commitments and spend a good deal of time outlining their structures. Class participants practice their newfound skills by making various working commitments to one another that follow a clear-cut lifecycle and structure. (See the following diagram.) To gain a greater understanding, I urge you to read more about the brilliant Fernando Flores's commitment theory by googling the numerous articles and discussions available online. (Fernando Flores is referenced in Chapters 5 and 7 of this book.)

BASIC ACTION WORKFLOW

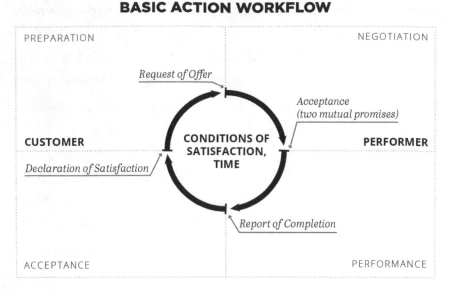

"Basic Action Workflow" by Dr. Fernando Flores and his colleagues is licensed under a Creative Commons Attribution 3.0 License. https://creativecommons.org/licenses/by/3.0/.

NO. 7—DETERMINE DECISION RIGHTS

Without a doubt, this can be one of the stickiest step of an experiment or implementation process, certainly in the effort to re-tool an existing bureaucratic hierarchy into a dynamic, self-managed network of title-free contributors, but also in a startup situation. That's because even a startup has to recruit its workforce from other enterprises, and human beings bring their previous work modes and habits—and their ingrained personality traits—with them when they walk in the door.

The long-and-short of it is that people can have trouble giving up power, status, rank, and privilege. Many have become so accustomed to being identified by such markers that they have lost confidence in their capacity to be valued on the basis of performance and ability to work with others. In a self-managed environment, decision rights are generally owned by those who are closest to the task at hand or who have the skill and expertise to properly assess results in a given area. In bureaucratic hierarchies, on the other hand, designated managers of others typically own the rights to make decisions, regardless of how close they are to the results. What's more, it is common for decision rights to be poorly defined in conventional workplaces or not defined at all, creating messiness and conflict.

Self-managed organizations recognize that an important component in ensuring the success of the enterprise is the ability to clearly define decision rights. Well-defined decision rights are crucial in self-management to ensure accountability. They can be negotiated and renegotiated as required, with the individual possessing the greatest level of expertise for a given area typically owning the decisions for that area. Self-management does not require a human "boss" because transparency and clarity of process ownership—plus related decision rights—make accountabilities clear. In a truly open, self-managed enterprise, there is no place to hide.

NO. 8—CREATE AND NURTURE FEEDBACK LOOPS

Self-management is all about the constant flow of feedback regarding behaviors, suggestions for continuous improvement, innovation, and more. The self-managed network continually rides along a giant feedback loop. In whatever manner the members of the enterprise can enable, support, ease, and improve the feedback loop process, that is how much more effective the process will be. That makes it worth dedicated thought and consideration at the onset of any self-management initiative. Which brings us to . . .

NO. 9—IDENTIFY AND INCORPORATE SOCIAL TECHNOLOGY SYSTEMS AND TOOLS

Social systems and tools are all about how people relate to one another. In the self-managed enterprise of today, new social tools and technologies help the organization to respect the voices of individuals and foster inclusion. After all, everyone, no matter how introverted, deserves the opportunity to be heard. Yet, such is not ordinarily possible in the traditional organization, where communication channels are constructed around presentations, meetings, and status reports. Endless opportunities for rich understanding and communication among peers is lost in such an environment. But with tools such as OpenSpace and The World Café, self-managers can ensure that everyone's voice is heard.

New means of enabling rich communication are cropping up regularly. Rod Collins, former chief operating executive of the Blue Cross Blue Shield Federal Employee Program and author of *Wiki Management: A Revolutionary New Model for a Rapidly Changing and Collaborative World,* shares an exercise he calls "The Elegant Set," a method of quickly aggregating the collective intelligence in a room of diverse stakeholders.[90] Keith McCandless and Henri Lipmanowicz, co-authors of *The Surprising Power of Liberating Structures: Simple Rules to Unleash A Culture of Innovation*, also describe several simple yet powerful exercises designed to unleash innovation and performance through engagement.[91]

To the degree that they are embraced and deployed, liberating social technologies will exert tectonic pressure on traditional organi-

---

90   Rod Collins, *Wiki Management: A Revolutionary New Model for a Rapidly Changing and Collaborative World* (New York: AMACOM, 2014).

91   Keith McCandless and Henri Lipmanowicz, *The Surprising Power of Liberating Structures: Simple Rules to Unleash A Culture of Innovation* (Seattle: Liberating Structures Press, 2013).

zations to, well, *liberate* people. Once exposed to these technologies, people will *expect* to have a voice and have that voice be heard.

NO. 10—DEFINE YOUR ENTERPRISE WORLDVIEW: START WITH PRINCIPLES

We have talked at length about the importance of an enterprise's statements of Principles, Philosophies, Core Values, and Constitution (or constitution-like document). Without clarity around what steers the enterprise, the company ship is rudderless, and any organizational structure (or non-structure, in the case of pure self-management) is built on quicksand. Furthermore, the peer agreements that are so central to the success of a self-managed enterprise (given their role in replacing costly bureaucracy) will have no foundation.

To put it plainly: the success of the peer agreements relies on the principles of the enterprise. Do people have free will? Is force or coercion acceptable? What is the importance of commitment? Can people manage themselves at work? Philosophy, as it turns out, is important! While many people are eager to jump directly to tools and practices, the better approach is to start with principles, and let principles guide the adoption of tools and practices.

> *To put it plainly: the success of the peer agreements relies on the principles of the enterprise.*

NO. 11—CREATE AN ENTERPRISE PEER AGREEMENT TEMPLATE

I believe that written Peer Agreements (what Morning Star calls the "Colleague Letter of Understanding" or CLOU) are extremely valuable in any implementation of self-management. They minimize ambiguity and help to ensure clarity and transparency, which are so key to high performance across an enterprise. But they also help to reduce the number of possible entry points for the destructive effects of non-delivery of responsibilities, disengagement, toxic influence, politicking, power-mongering, and the like. *The Peer Agreement is the organizational scaffolding that replaces bureaucracy and gives every contributor a voice.*

Importantly, the very process of having to carefully think through the peer agreement will help you and your colleagues to solidify the vision of a self-managed workplace, now shared across the enterprise

A peer agreement can be whatever you want it to be. There is no one model for peer agreements, but all peer agreements should incorporate by reference the enterprise's statement(s) of principles and philosophies, including the mission and purpose of the enterprise. Following are two examples of templates used by companies I have worked with.

Template [1] is an example of a simple document that leaves little to self-interpretation so that the business of the enterprise can hum along fairly unimpeded. This peer agreement can be easily amended to accommodate new or additional rings of responsibility, as needed.

Template [2] is a more visual approach to a peer agreement, shown as a "canvas" with each contributor's purpose at the center.

PEER AGREEMENT

NAME:

DATE:

NETWORK COLLEAGUES:

PURPOSE:

1. Why do I want to work here?
2. What does excellence look like in my role?
3. How does what I do support the mission of this enterprise?

PROCESS ACCOUNTABILITY COMMITMENTS

DECISION RIGHTS

SCORECARDS

PLANNING

ORGANIZING

CONTROLLING

SELECTING

COORDINATING

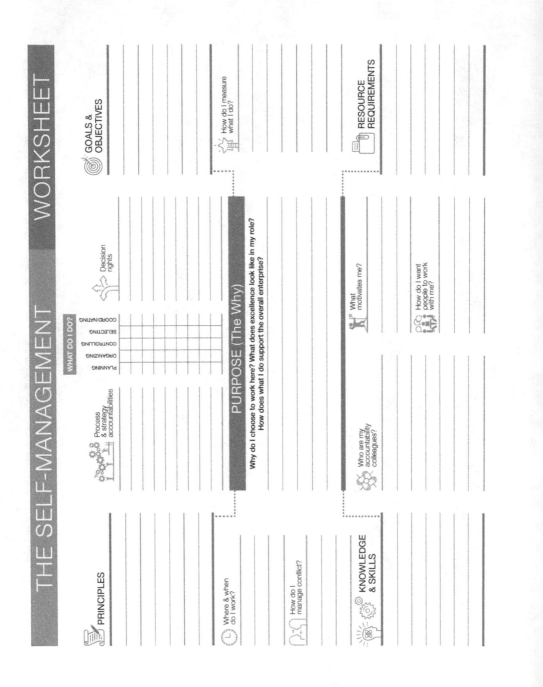

THE SELF-MANAGEMENT WORKSHEET

PRINCIPLES

Process & strategy accountabilities

WHAT DO I DO?

PLANNING
ORGANIZING
CONTROLLING
SELECTING
COORDINATING

Decision rights

GOALS & OBJECTIVES

How do I measure what I do?

Where & when do I work?

How do I manage conflict?

PURPOSE (The Why)

Why do I choose to work here? What does excellence look like in my role?
How does what I do support the overall enterprise?

Who are my accountability colleagues?

What motivates me?

How do I want people to work with me?

KNOWLEDGE & SKILLS

RESOURCE REQUIREMENTS

In addition to developing Peer Agreements, leaders must to perform the unavoidably hard work of developing supportable processes for conflict management, hiring and firing, compensation and other functions which incorporate the values and principles of their self-managed, No-Limits Enterprise.

NO. 12—CREATE A STRUCTURE FOR LEARNING AND DEVELOPMENT (SUSTAINMENT)

Providing a learning and development platform can help to amplify the self-management skills people may already possess, and also help them develop business know-how. As I have pointed out earlier, this kind of education also serves to help self-management sustain and perpetuate itself as new hires come on board and people move about the network of teams and functions as needed.

Morning Star graduated several colleague cohorts from its Mini MBA program, detailed in Chapter 8, which offered courses and modules in strategy, business process management, financial literacy, and general business skills (negotiation, mediation, interviewing, leadership, and teamwork). It was a holistic approach, offering skills development (for example, in strategy) that could be holistically applied both to one's work and personal life.

Your educational platform—even if it launches with just a course or two—can be designed internally or with outside help to meet the demands and needs of enterprise stakeholders. Think about the learning requirements of a sustainable self-management ecosystem in your enterprise. Consider starting a book club to build interest, dialogue, and momentum (a microcosm "exercise" that mirrors Stephenie Gloden's approach) and you may be surprised by the amount of human energy that is released. People love to share what they know with others, to help them avoid re-inventing wheels that are already rolling. Encourage learners to teach others—it embeds the learning more deeply.

And don't forget about technology: with the proliferation of Learning Management Systems (LMS), adaptive learning platforms, and microlearning, the only educational limit on the No-Limits Enterprise is the sky.

CONCLUSION

MAKING "NO LIMITS" YOUR REALITY

Success is not the key to happiness. Happiness is the key to success. If you love what you are doing, you will be successful.

—Albert Schweitzer, theologian, writer, humanitarian, philosopher, and physician

LOOK AT THE QUOTATION above and multiply it by the number of employees you have currently, or the number with which you will launch your new venture. Whether it's a startup with fifty employees, or a global enterprise with 50,000, can you imagine that workplace with close to 100 percent engagement? An enterprise populated by genuinely happy people who like, love, or enjoy what they do in the two-thirds of life that many people only slog through to get to retirement?

That is the kind of enterprise that forward-thinking business leaders envision. They know that an enterprise that continuously feeds its own network of engaged, connected, enthusiastic contributors and innovators is an enterprise that is unconstrained by the ills of yesterday's command-and-control organizational hierarchies. It is an enterprise that, with excellence as its benchmark and beacon, can achieve virtually anything its constituents can dream up. It is a No-Limits Enterprise.

No Limits, Straight Ahead

In this book, we have seen how the breakdown of bureaucracy in the workplace means that the future is no longer something business leaders can only muse about. The future is here, right now, and it is moving at exponentially greater speed every year.

We have envisaged a vast parade of human talent and enthusiasm for collaboration and innovation that is available to the enterprise, yet has been ill-used to the wasteful disadvantage of *both* working humans and the business world at large.

We've looked at the modern drivers of "flattening" in domestic and global corporations, and various workforce models that exist along a continuum stretching all the way from slavery, through flattened governance structures, to pure self-management.

We've visited real-world implementations of self-management that include some of the most innovative and successful companies in the world, businesses both mammoth and small, domestic and global, previously entrenched in crumbling bureaucracy or starting up from scratch. We've looked at thriving, purely self-managed organizations, companies that have opted for modified versions of self-governance, even companies that have launched forms of self-governance that now need to be reassessed.

Within a powerful Self-Management Roadmap, we have considered all-important talking points to help any company leader or leadership team to make the case for self-management to enterprise stakeholders. And as any good roadmap does, we have provided the basic directions to get from here to there. Yet, what of the landmarks or obstacles along the way?

We've addressed common (and not so common) FAQs, and have thought through the countless considerations for, and implications of, self-management. We've also moved you, the business leader or owner, through a process of self-assessment, both personal and corporate. It is a process essential to any successful transition to self-management. No radical organizational change with all the promise that self-management holds can be successful without a thoroughly committed leader or leaders at the helm. Self-management, in particular, requires visionary people who understand that humanity and great business are inextricably entwined.

Most importantly, a true visionary knows that companies, organizations, and teams are concepts (even countries are concepts), but when it comes to business, individual human beings are the only things that are *real*. They consume products and services, build and create things, imagine things, and endlessly innovate. So, if business is all about human beings, then don't we need to care about them, support them, and nurture them for all they give back to us and to the world at large? When we do that, and, consequently, deliver products and services to the marketplace that have been produced with passion, care, and love, we are rewarded by a marketplace that lifts us higher and higher. Most of all, we are lifted by a common good and a striving for excellence that the world so urgently needs right now.

In the simplest terms, self-management is the clear path to the vastly more human workplace that is long overdue. Happily, for the prescient business leader, self-

Self-management is the clear path to the vastly more human workplace that is long overdue.

management is also the means to an enterprise that will know no limits to success because it is no longer bound by useless bureaucracy. There has never been a better time to seize the day and embrace a future that rewards courage in leadership. *Carpe diem.*

Some Final Thoughts

I think back to those many years ago when my first-grade teacher asked us to color with a brown crayon and I decided to use black and brown crayons instead and was summarily reprimanded. As I shared early on in this book, I've been fascinated by the tension between organizational freedom and accountability ever since, and have learned that organizational self-management is real, it works, and it drives superior business performance.

Now, I enjoy sharing what I've learned with leaders all across the US and in every corner of the globe; from Shanghai to Stockholm, Serbia to Siberia, Sao Paulo to San Antonio. The opportunity to engage in lifelong learning and share it with others is my passion.

I also believe that we practitioners stand on the shoulders of giants: people such as Dr. Peter Koestenbaum (philosopher of freedom and accountability at work), Fernando Flores (theoretician of artificial intelligence and speech acts), and Dee Hock (founder of Visa, author, and organizational thinker), plus many other pioneers. For all those shoulders, I am grateful.

My dream is that current and future generations will be able to view work as an energizing, vibrant part of life and not as something one has to do to in order to make money to retire. I welcome contact with all those who share that dream. If this topic interests you and you want to learn more, please feel free to reach out on LinkedIn, Twitter, or at www.nufocusgroupusa.com.

ABOUT THE AUTHOR

Growing up in Northwest Montana afforded many opportunities to explore and manage the polarities of freedom and accountability. Working on wheat farms, cattle ranches, and campgrounds seemed to occupy most of my time not spent in school.

After college, I was privileged to serve as the first financial controller for Morning Star, which grew from nothing to become the world's largest tomato processing company; its products consumed by nearly everyone in North America and millions more around the world. Our founder introduced the startup team to the core principles of organizational self-management, which we adopted immediately. At Morning Star, I learned that organizational self-management is real, it works, and it drives superior business performance.

Over the years I've been privileged to serve on multiple hard-working boards and have a deep appreciation for their consequential stewardship and fiduciary responsibility. These boards include: the Merced County Workforce Investment Board, the boards of directors for the Professional Coaches and Mentors Association, the Association for Talent Development, the Manufacturer's Council of the Central Valley, the Children's Services Network and others. Each board was an incredible learning experience.

In 2012, I began speaking and consulting on self-management throughout North America and in nearly forty countries around the world. I also share the message of organizational innovation through my books (*Beyond Empowerment: The Age of the Self-Managed Organization* and *From Hierarchy to High Performance: Unleashing the Hidden Superpowers of Ordinary People to Realize Extraordinary*

Results), TEDx talk, and articles in *The Huffington Post Blog* on Great Work Cultures.

Former business partner Suzanne Daigle, co-author with Harrison Owen and others of *Forum Ouvert* (the French guide to Open Space Technology), heard one of those talks and invited me to join NuFocus, a full-spectrum international consulting firm born in Canada. Our mission was simple: we wanted to help our clients create thriving, high-performing cultures where people were free to do their best work.

For me and the inspiring partners around the world with whom I collaborate, that mission continues without ceasing.

A PASSION FOR FREEDOM AND ACCOUNTABILITY AT WORK

Work cultures appear to be at a tipping point in making the case for transcending outdated bureaucracies—interest is bubbling all around the world about the benefits of creating engaging workplaces where everyone has a voice. Workplaces that inspire and liberate people, and respect the inherent adulthood of contributors, will have a strategic competitive advantage in the future of work. We're rapidly moving beyond theory into real-world examples.

Our hope is that this book will help accelerate the appreciation of these realities by leaders who can make a difference. We recently returned from China where an apparel manufacturing CEO declared his intent to convert his entire 3,000-person workforce to a self-managed ecosystem, where people are fully accountable to each other—not to bosses on an org chart.

We're always happy to connect with anyone who wants to learn how to make organizations thrive with engaged, innovative, and self-directed leaders. To contact us, visit our website at https://dougkirkpatrick.com.

OUR SERVICES

NuFocus Strategic Group provides trusted advisement regarding organizational design and development, coaching, mentoring, education, and training. Our mission is to help our clients have accountable people make the right decisions, manage risk appropriately, and effectively engage the hearts and minds of all contributors with responsible freedom. We want our clients to be winners, to thrive, and to grow.

We also want our clients to be able to align their business strategies with effective people strategies in order to create a culture that powerfully translates those strategies into actions.

NuFocus helps clients implement organizational self-management through culture, systems, language, technologies, principles, and practices to make their businesses thrive.

Our expertise includes:

- Organizational Self-Management Implementation
- Self-Management Masterclasses and Workshops
- Networked Organization Software
- Open Space Technology
- Agile Beyond Software
- Conference Design and Development
- Keynote Speaking
- Culture Change
- Leadership Development
- Organizational Assessment

LinkedIn: https://www.linkedin.com/in/redshifter3

Twitter: @Redshifter3

Web: http://www.nufocusgroupusa.com

Blog: https://www.redshift3.org

A PASSION FOR FREEDOM AND ACCOUNTABILITY AT WORK

Work cultures appear to be at a tipping point in making the case for transcending outdated bureaucracies—interest is bubbling all around the world about the benefits of creating engaging workplaces where everyone has a voice. Workplaces that inspire and liberate people, and respect the inherent adulthood of contributors, will have a strategic competitive advantage in the future of work. We're rapidly moving beyond theory into real-world examples.

Our hope is that this book will help accelerate the appreciation of these realities by leaders who can make a difference. We recently returned from China where an apparel manufacturing CEO declared his intent to convert his entire 3,000-person workforce to a self-managed ecosystem, where people are fully accountable to each other—not to bosses on an org chart.

We're always happy to connect with anyone who wants to learn how to make organizations thrive with engaged, innovative, and self-directed leaders.

To contact us, visit our website at

http://www.nufocusgroupusa.com,

e-mail **d.kirkpatrick@nufocusgroup.com**,

or call **209.605.5869**.

Printed in the USA
CPSIA information can be obtained
at www.ICGtesting.com
JSHW021425300124
56347JS00001B/26